ORGANISING EFFECTIVE TRAINING

BUSINESS BASICS

ORGANISING EFFECTIVE TRAINING

How to plan and run
successful courses and seminars

James Chalmers

ARE YOU NODDING IN AGREEMENT, OR FALLING ASLEEP?

How To Books

Cartoons by Mike Flanagan

British Library Cataloguing in Publication Data
A catalogue record for this book is available from the British Library.

© Copyright 1996 by James Chalmers.

First published in 1996 by How To Books Ltd, Plymbridge House, Estover
Road, Plymouth PL6 7PZ, United Kingdom. Tel: (01752) 202301.
Fax: (01752) 202331.

Note: The material contained in this book is set out in good faith for
general guidance and no liability can be accepted for loss or expense
incurred as a result of relying in particular circumstances on statements
made in the book. The laws and regulations are complex and liable to
change, and readers should check the current position with the relevant
authorities before making personal arrangements.

Produced for How To Books by Deer Park Productions.
Typeset by PDQ Typesetting, Stoke-on-Trent, Staffs.
Printed and bound by Cromwell Press, Broughton Gifford, Melksham,
Wiltshire.

Contents

5

List of Illustrations

Preface

With today's emphasis on customer care and service as the way to move forward and gain an edge over competitors, training is an essential part of business development. In any organisation effective training will enhance performance, and consequently ensure success and increase profitability.

Effective training isn't something that just happens by itself. There is, however, no real mystery to it. *Good organisation* is the key to success.

Training doesn't have to be tedious and boring. The most effective training is often light-hearted, and always includes a variety of interesting sessions, involving staff and making them feel part of the team.

Training doesn't have to be costly either. Any outlay will soon be recouped in benefits to the company.

Throughout the book you will find lots of ideas for different techniques, materials and presentation aids; for example brainstorming, quizzes and videos. I hope you will find many of these useful in your own training events.

Good luck with your training efforts, and remember that as long as you plan carefully you will have a successful outcome every time.

James Chalmers

IS THIS YOU?

Small business manager

Production shop manager

Training manager

Customer service team manager

Building society manager

Teacher

Repair department manager

Adult education tutor

Emergency services instructor

Local government officer

Security company manager

Personnel manager

Trades union official

Hospital manager

Cultural organisation official

Drama school teacher

Secretarial skills tutor

Voluntary organisation officer

Retail manager

Gallery manager

Church leader

Youth club leader

Tourist attraction manager

Leisure centre manager

Zoo manager

Sales team leader

Lecturer

Bank manager

Enterprise centre manager

Armed services instructor

Transport company manager

Safety manager

Disabled centre manager

Community group leader

Museum manager

Hotel manager

Arts and crafts demonstrator

Holiday site organiser

1
Getting Off to a Good Start

PLANNING FOR SUCCESS

Training a person, or a group of people, means adding something to their existing skills or knowledge, as in Figure 1. The **training** in the box in Figure 1 could be something very short and simple, or it might last several days. In this book, it is always referred to as a **training event**, whatever the length or method used.

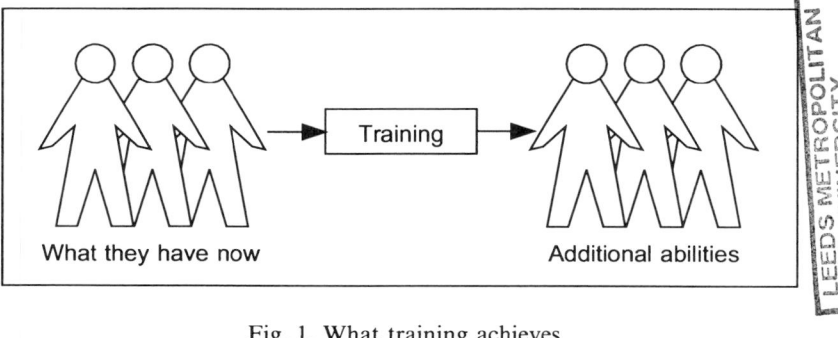

Fig. 1. What training achieves

A well organised training event is the key to effective training. Designing a training event, provided it's done carefully is quite straightforward. This book describes a step-by-step approach which is logical and easy to follow.

LOOKING AT DIFFERENT SITUATIONS

Let's start by looking at the different situations where there is a need for training. In many of the examples you will notice the two-word phrase *so that*. This is a simple way of looking ahead to when the training has been completed. It's what the delegates will have gained as a result of attending the training event.

11

Changing to something new

If a working practice is changed the knowledge of an already skilled workforce will need to be added to, *so that* they can continue to operate effectively.

Example
The accounts department is to have a new computer system installed. Staff will need to be trained to use the computer.

Starting a new job

People taking up a new job, or moving to another department, will need to be trained in all aspects of the work they are to do *so that* they can make an effective contribution to the work of their employer.

Example
A graduate is recruited to run a tele-sales team. She will need management and sales skills training.

Refreshing existing skills

People doing a job for a long time may need training at regular intervals *so that* the standard of their work is maintained.

Example
Police armed response units carrying guns on routine patrols will need regular practice with their weapons. A weekly visit to the firing range, supervised by a qualified instructor, may be required.

Programming regular training

Many companies have long-term programmes of training *so that* effective team working continues.

Example
Technicians assembling business telephone systems, in a medium-sized factory, having regular monthly training events. These could include how to get the best out of new tools and equipment, and items to build good team working.

Fighting fires

This is the least acceptable approach to the identification of training needs. It means waiting for something to go wrong, then having a training event *so that* it corrects the situation.

Example
Customers have been complaining about the behaviour of a delivery driver. Send him on a customer care course to teach him to be polite and courteous.

Making money
You can run training events as a business. You identify where you think there is a training need, design a training event and advertise it. People will pay to attend.

Example
A one-day seminar, run in a local hotel, on how small businesses can introduce quality improvement techniques.

Teaching students
Universities, colleges, schools, teaching hospitals and other places for formal education are training people, even though it is usually called teaching. Lectures and classes, laboratory sessions and field activities, can all be planned using the methods described in this book.

Example
A ten-week course on first aid in the home, run by the St John Ambulance organisation.

DECIDING IF THERE IS A TRAINING NEED

To decide if there is a need for training write down a few lines to describe the situation. Divide this under the following two headings:

• What are they doing now?   • What should they be doing?

Examples

What are they doing now?	What should they be doing?
The accounts team are making a lot of mistakes.	They should be making no mistakes at all.
The police officers in country areas are unfamiliar with drugs, which until recently were confined to towns and cities.	They should be able to recognise and identify all types of drugs in current use in the UK and abroad.

The council road repair workmen have been criticised by the Health and Safety Executive over their inadequate use of warning signs. They must be able to set out road works guarding in accordance with legal requirements.

By writing notes in this way the difference between the *now* and *should be* situations become more apparent. When there is a difference between what the two statements are saying there is a need for training.

DEFINING RESPONSIBILITIES

Once a need for training has been identified, someone must design and deliver a training event. Let's look at who is involved. Figure 2 is a flow chart showing the training process from the identification of the need, through to the delivery of the training at the event.

The best way to understand what everyone does is to start at the bottom of the chart and work up.

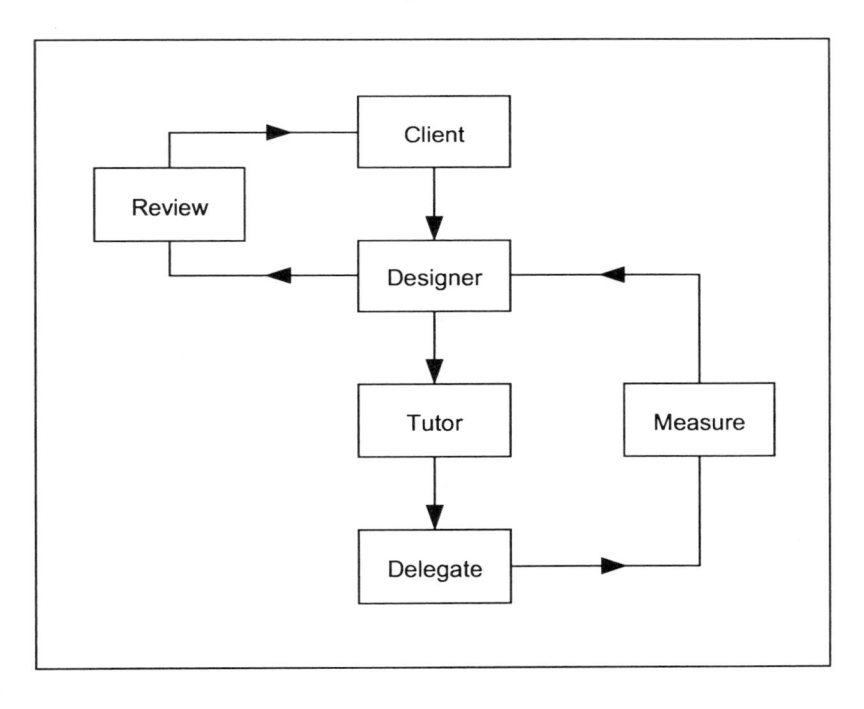

Fig. 2. Flow chart showing who is involved with training.

Attending the event: the delegates

The **delegates** are the people who attend the event. They come away at the end with their skills or knowledge increased to the required level. Delegates are often referred to as:

- students
- trainees
- attendees
- pupils
- class members
- candidates
- team members.

Delivering the training: the tutor

The **tutor** delivers the training to the delegates. Sometimes there is a leader, with other people acting as tutors for the various sessions that make up the event. The tutor may also be the event **designer** in some cases.

Tutors may also be known as:

- trainers
- facilitators
- presenters
- lecturers
- instructors
- event leaders
- teachers.

Planning everything: the designer

The designer is the person who plans everything, from the content of the various event sessions to the booking of training rooms and hotel accommodation. The designer may also be the **client** in some situations.

Some companies will have official titles for people whose job it is to organise training. Typical names are:

- course organisers
- event planners
- training managers
- change managers.

Saying what's required: the client

The client is the person responsible for identifying the training need. He/she then passes details of his/her requirements to the designer.

Internal Memo

From: Tim Marlborough   To: Brian Jones
       Factory Manager   Service Dept

5.2.9X

The company is adopting a new approach to dealing with customer complaints. From 2nd April your team will have access to the main customer database, and all staff will be expected to deal with any letters of complaint referred to them. This means logging the information into the system and writing suitable replies.

Can you please organise some suitable training, so that everyone is able to work with the new system when it comes on line.

I think a one-day course will suffice.

Tim Marlborough
Factory Manager

Notes scribbled on an A4 pad   12.5.9X

Several complaints about one of my drivers, Dave. Customers say he's rather rude to them.

This was mentioned to him last year. He promised to improve. That hasn't happened.

Organise some training. A half day should be enough.

Bring in other drivers so that Dave doesn't feel he's being singled out.

Needs to be about caring for our customers, so that all my drivers, including Dave, know how to be courteous to customers.

Fred Arkle
Manager, Arkle's Prompt Deliveries

Fig. 3. Examples of client requirements.

16

Because the client starts off the whole process his or her role is very important. We will look at what the client needs to do to get things off to a good start.

WRITING DOWN THE CLIENT REQUIREMENTS

The starting point for organising effective training is the client telling the designer exactly what is required. In all cases it is important for the client to record his or her requirements by writing them down. This is the starting point for a well designed training event. The client requirements can either be handwritten, typed or printed from a personal computer.

Two examples of written client requirements are illustrated in Figure 3.

Saying what is required
Both clients in Figure 3 are saying they want some training organised to achieve a specified goal.

There are no firm rules as to how you should record the client's requirements. Each situation will be different, but here are some key points:

• State what the training must achieve.

• Say who the training is for.

• Give any other background or helpful information.

• Record on paper or a computer disk.

• Identify by a date and the client's name.

Marking the client requirements with a name and date
A name and date on the client requirements are important. The name identifies who the client is, and if the client requirements are changed after discussions the updated version will not be confused with the original notes.

Building up a file
It is advisable to build up a file of information for each training event you design. The written client requirements is the first item in the file.

The advantages of having a file of information are:

- It helps to establish a logical approach.

- You have something to take to the client when you review the progress of the design.

- You have something to base changes on after you have run the initial event.

- If you need to run a similar event in the future you can refer back to the original event file.

COMPLETING THE PICTURE

The flow chart in Figure 2 has two other boxes: Review and Measure.

Reviewing with the client
The review box indicates the discussions between the designer and the client, to make sure that the event being planned is what the client actually wants.

Measuring success
If you design and run training events, based on the advice given in this book, you can be confident of a successful outcome. But it is still very comforting to have the proof of success, just to confirm your own feelings about how things went on the day.

You measure success by comparing what was intended to happen with what actually happened.

CHECKLIST FOR PRODUCING CLIENT REQUIREMENTS

First steps to designing a training event
1. Decide if there is a training need.
    (a) Write down what they are doing now.
    (b) Write down what they should be doing.
    (c) If the statements differ there is a training need.

2. Write down the client requirements.
    (a) Can be formal or informal.
    (b) State what the training is to achieve.
    (c) Write on paper or computer disk.
    (d) Include client's name and the date.
    (e) Say who is to be trained.

(f) If known, suggest length of training and other ideas.

(g) Pass this to designer.

3. Set up a file. Include the client requirements as the first item.

CASE STUDIES

Now meet three companies we will be looking at in subsequent chapters. Although their businesses are quite different they share the need to organise effective training for their employees.

Michael's muddled approach makes for problems

A local authority accounts department, consisting of five teams each with its own manager, is responsible for the receipt of payments for a wide variety of activities, from the hire of rooms for WI meetings to the collection of business rates.

There are around ninety clerical-grade staff, full time and agency, operating with an out-of-date computer system. The work is dull and repetitive, and the office is located in a bland 1960s building. Staff morale is low, sick leave absence is unacceptably high, and the error rate for the input of payment details is running at fifteen per cent. To add to the feeling of gloom there are strong rumours about the whole payment activity being subcontracted to a local banking firm.

Michael, a qualified accountant, has overall charge of the department. He is good with figures, but lacks basic management skills training. His monthly meetings with the team managers, for example, are poorly structured, long-winded and boring.

Joyce is one of Michael's team managers. She has a good understanding of how the computer system works and has a logical approach to all aspects of her work. She never misses running the Monday morning half-hour briefing session with her team, and will always undertake follow-up briefings with anyone who was absent.

The local authority does have its own training department and a generous training budget which is usually underspent each year. One of the full-time trainers, Jackie, has been allocated to the accounts department, but she is rarely active in this area.

Michael has not recognised the importance of training. He believes he can leave it to his team managers to sort out the department's problem.

Peter's expert planning keeps his customers happy

Peter owns three independent high street shops, specialising in quality TV, video and audio equipment. He faces fierce competition from the larger retail chains, particularly those in the out of town retail parks. His main defence is his reputation for excellent customer service.

Having well-trained staff is the key to maintaining a lead over Peter's bigger rivals. Their knowledge of the products must be kept up to date, and their customer-care skills second to none. An additional complication is the use of a subcontractor for the home delivery of the larger items. This is a small local transport firm whose delivery people have to be able to set up and demonstrate the equipment to the customers, as well as being reliable and polite.

Peter can't afford a full-time trainer, and has no special training rooms or facilities at any of his shops. In spite of this he has managed to plan and organise effective training, both for his own people and the subcontractors.

Geraldine leads the troops

Charles is the branch manager of a building society. He is also a captain in the Royal Marine Reserves, and spends most weekends away on military exercises. In his role as a marine he has been trained in all the skills of a commando, and is well respected by his subordinate officers and men.

At the building society, however, he stays in the office, out of sight of the customers. He prefers to leave most of the day-to-day organisation to one of his customer advisers, Geraldine. Charles has been trained in all the duties of the customer adviser, including using the computer system. He is also the main contact for mortgage advice, but again he likes to leave that to Geraldine.

When Geraldine isn't around and there's a difficult customer to deal with, or an unusual enquiry, he does not fully understand what he is supposed to do.

The area manager who overseas a dozen branches has noticed Charles's lack of involvement. She cannot understand why, after all the training he has received, he can't manage the job he is being paid for.

DISCUSSION POINTS

1. Think about some training you have experienced as a delegate which was not particularly effective. Do you think badly written client requirements could have been the root cause of the problem?

2. If you were asked to give an after-dinner speech on a subject of your choice, at a local charity event, what items do you think would appear in the client requirements?

3. You know the importance of the client requirements being the first item in the designer's file. If you were the client as well as the designer might there be additional advantages in filing preliminary notes?

2
Sorting Out the Building Blocks

SETTING THE EVENT OBJECTIVE

You now know what the client wants. The next step is to turn the client requirements into the **event objective.**

Although the value of having a clear event objective is very important, setting it is relatively simple.

Writing out the event objective

The event objective is a description of what the training event will achieve, plus other information such as who the training is for.

A description of the event is written out as follows.

Event title   This is just an identity label at this stage and can be changed later as the design evolves.

Duration   A rough estimate which can be changed as the design evolves.

Who for   Department, people, etc.

A 'to' statement   Why the event is being run.

A 'so that' statement What the delegates will gain.

Working from the client requirements

In some situations the event designer will be able to use the client requirements word for word, but this will only apply if the client has been formal and precise.

In most cases the client requirements may be too sketchy to use them directly as the event objective, so this means the designer having to add more detail.

When setting the event objective:

• Read and understand the client requirements.

- Write out the objective as a personal view of what the training event is to achieve in order to meet the client requirements.

- Include as many items as considered necessary after the 'so that' phrase.

Three examples of written event objectives are illustrated in Figure 4.

EVENT OBJECTIVES

Handling customer complaints
A one-day course for non-managers in the service department

to: familiarise them with the new complaint handling
               procedures

so that: they will be able to log complaints on the database, and
               deal with the customers on all aspects of the company's
               products and services, including writing replies.

Team building seminar
A two-day event for the new accounts department team

to: get to know each other

so that: the efficiency of the department is enhanced by their ability
               to work as one team.

Workmanship checks
A half-day meeting for production team managers

to: explain the new method of sampling quality levels

so that: team managers can undertake checks, record the results,
               take corrective action and submit monthly reports.

Fig. 4. Examples of written event objectives.

Estimating the duration of the event

The duration is an important part of the event description. Potential delegates will not only want to know what it's all about, but how long it will take. At this stage the duration is only a rough estimate, based on one or more of the following:

- a guess by the event designer
- imposed by the client or an accountant
- suggested by the delegates based on how much time they'll have available
- experience of similar events
- availability of venues, travelling time, etc.

You will find yourself going round a few loops before you come to a conclusion about the duration. This may also include quite a bit of negotiation with the client.

TRYING OUT AN INITIAL REVIEW

When you have written the event objective, in the 'to/so that' form, you should take it to the client and ask if it is what they had in mind.

There is no point in continuing to develop an event with an objective that doesn't match the client's aims. Be prepared to put a line through your first effort if the response is negative.

Reviewing the objective without a client

If you are arranging the event on your own behalf, show the written objective to one or more of the following:

- A friend, or someone you work with. Ask them to say what they think it means. They should interpret your statement in a way that sounds like what you have in mind.

- One of the people who will be coming to the event as a delegate. They should be able to confirm that it will meet their expectations.

- The person in the organisation who will be authorising the expenditure. They should be able to give you an opinion as to whether it's justified on economic grounds.

Getting the message across

The objective of a training event is there as much for the delegates as it is for the designer and client. It tells the delegates why they are being trained and what the training event is all about.

Never try to get a hidden message across at a training event, by having an objective that is not honest. The delegates are likely to spot the deception and hit back by disrupting the event.

Filing the event objective

Chapter 1 recommended you to set up a file of information for each event you design. Once the event objective has been agreed with the client a copy should be filed immediately after the client requirements.

It's wise to file all papers relating to the design of training events, as we shall see later on.

BUILDING THE EVENT WITH SESSIONS

Once the event objective has been agreed, the next step is to build the event with **sessions**.

Building with blocks

Building a training event is like making a tower from children's toy bricks. This is illustrated in Figure 5.

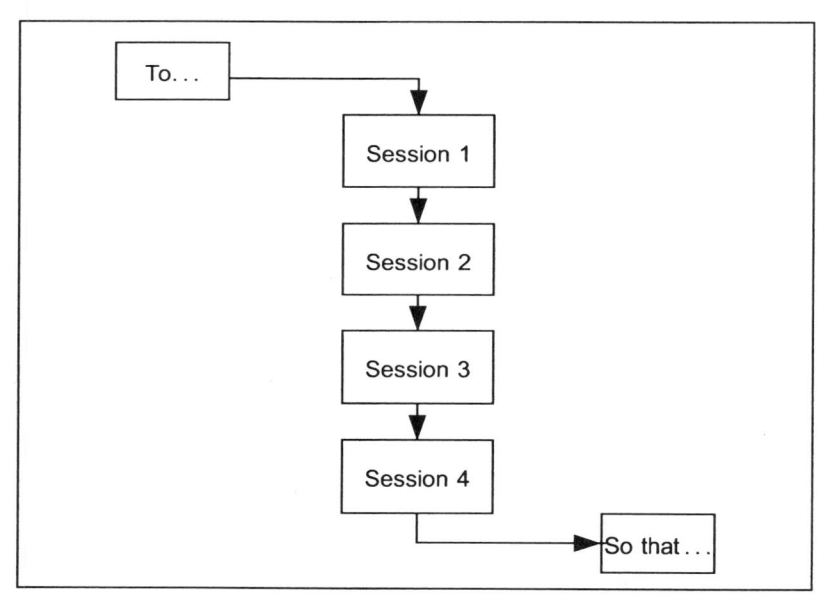

Fig. 5. A training event is built with sessions.

HANDLING CUSTOMER COMPLAINTS

Session	'To'	'So that'	'How'
1. Policy	Define company policy	Delegates understand company policy and customers' rights	Presentation by director of customer service
2. Computer system	Explain computer logging system	Delegates can log in complaints search for information and back-up system	Hands-on with terminals in training room
3. Letter writing theory	Teach delegates the art of letter writing	They know how to reply in a courteous and effective manner	Presentation by personal assistant to customer relations manager
4. Letter writing practice	Allow delegates to practice letter writing	Tutor and delegates have confidence that message has been conveyed in session 3	Syndicate exercise with dummy complaints
5. Stats	Explain monitoring process	Delegates will understand how complaint levels will be measured	Presentation by statistics manager

Fig. 6. An example of a session list.

Going from the start to the end

At the start of the event the tutor and the delegates will have a clear idea of what the aims of the event are from the 'to' statement in the objective.

The event itself is made up of a number of sessions covering different topics. The sessions are run one at a time. By the end of the event all the delegates will have reached their goal, the 'so that' part of the objective.

To get a clearer idea of what this means in practice look at the three examples of objectives in Figure 4. Imagine the 'to' statements at the starting point, and the 'so that' statements at the end, for each objective in turn.

Listing the sessions

Deciding what each session should be is a similar exercise to setting the event objective. You use the 'to' and 'so that' form again, and add in a 'how'.

Introductory sessions and meal breaks will be added later. At this stage all that's being considered are the working sessions. An example of a session list is illustrated in Figure 6.

Arriving at the session list

To arrive at the session list you should:

1. Think about the event objective. What steps will be required to go from 'to' to 'so that'?

2. Write down all the topics needed to be covered. In the example of handling customer complaints (Figure 6) the topics are:

   - policy

   - computer system

   - letters

   - statistics.

3. Further divide the topics if necessary. Letter writing is divided into theory and practice.

4. Fill in 'to', 'so that' and 'how' for each session, and number them consecutively.

Knowing where to start

It's easier to start with the 'how' and then go back to the 'to' and 'so that'. This is because you may already have a few ideas about the availability of items such as computers.

The range of materials available for the 'how' part of the session list is covered later in the book.

Obtaining help with the session list

If you are fairly knowledgeable in the subject to be covered by the event, sorting out the session list by this method will be relatively simple. However, if you're in the dark about most or even one part of it the following ideas will help.

• Ask the client what he or she thinks the sessions might be, and use this as your starting point.

• Discuss with experts in the department where the delegates will be working after the event. Ask them what they think needs to be covered.

• Look at a department already doing the work. List all the things you'd need to understand before you could work there. For example, if you had to write letters to customers what would you need from a training event to make you feel confident to be able to manage on your own?

REVIEWING THE SESSION LIST WITH THE CLIENT

When you have arrived at your session list, take it to the client and ask if they agree that it will meet the event objective.

Be prepared to go back to the drawing board if it's not what he or she had in mind.

If there isn't a client use one of the alternatives suggested under **Trying Out an Initial Review**.

CHECKLIST FOR EVENT OBJECTIVE AND WORKING SESSIONS

Setting the event objective and building the event from working sessions to meet the objective can be summarised by the following checklist:

1. Write out the event objective.
   (a) The event title.
   (b) An estimate of the duration.
   (c) Who the event is for.
   (d) A 'to/so that' statement.

2. Review with client and amend as necessary. File copy of agreed objective.

3. Divide into sessions.
   (a) List all the topics that will need to be covered.
   (b) Divide into theory and practice sessions.
   (c) Decide 'how' each session will be delivered.
   (d) Against each 'how' statement add 'to' and 'so that' statements.

4. Review with client and amend as necessary. File a copy of agreed session list.

CASE STUDIES

Michael's game-playing upsets the professionals

A local authority wants to reduce the errors being made by their accounts department clerical staff. The chief executive designs a checklist to be used by team managers to undertake random samples of the work done by their staff. He sends this to Michael, the head of the accounts department, and asks him to introduce it to the team managers using a half-day training event. He leaves the design of the training event for Michael to organise.

Michael asks Jackie, a training manager, to design and run a half-day course. He also gives her on paper his ideas of what he thinks each session should cover, and he suggests the event is called Managing Your Team More Professionally.

Michael thinks the concept of checklists will be unpopular. His plan is to use a series of team games at the event, so that the team managers will come up with the idea for these checks themselves. However, some of the delegates have already heard rumours about the checks and during the event they deliberately avoid coming to the conclusion that Michael wants. By the time the last session takes place, which covers how to fill in the checklists, the delegates have lost interest and can see no point in carrying out the checks.

Back with their teams they make very little effort to use the checking process properly.

Delighted customers play Peter's timely video game

Most of the video recorders Peter sells through his three high street shops can be programmed from the video plus numbers given in publications such as the *Radio Times*.

Peter designs a very simple training event, with an objective to demonstrate video plus programming of video recorders, so that the users can do it for themselves.

There are only two very short sessions. The first is the tutor showing how it's done from a copy of *Radio Times*. The second is the users trying it for themselves.

This simple idea works well. Peter starts as the tutor to some of his shop staff. Then they become the tutors who train the remaining staff. They also train the delivery people who have to demonstrate the equipment to the customers in their homes.

At each delivery of a video a free copy of the *Radio Times* is given to the customer. The delivery person then runs through the same training with the customer, to make sure they understand how to use their new video recorder. The customers are delighted because they have the confidence to use the video plus facility and have also received a free *Radio Times*.

Charles's good idea nearly ends in failure

The building society area manager writes to all the branch managers under her control, asking them to come up with ideas for improving general housekeeping behind the counters. She has noticed a lack of concern at many of the branches over the disposal of rubbish, messy kitchens and personal items such as handbags being left in places where others could trip over them.

Charles, who has military experience with the Royal Marine Reserves, suggests there should be random weekly inspections.

The area manager thinks Charles's suggestion is the best. She writes down her client requirements and asks him to design some training, lasting about an hour, to introduce all staff to good housekeeping practises, so that poor housekeeping is eliminated.

Charles writes out an objective, then compiles a session list. At this point the area manager asks to see what progress he has made. This is a timely intervention because Charles has concentrated on the inspections rather than the housekeeping. The area manager wants some inspections, but with the encouragement of good housekeeping to be the main theme. Charles is a little disappointed, but agrees to re-write the objective. This time it's accepted and he goes on to work on the sessions list.

At each stage of the design Charles makes sure he shows it to his manager. He realises it would be a waste of time to design a training event, however simple or short, if it was not what the client wanted.

The event is run at all branches and as a result a significant improvement in general housekeeping is observed.

DISCUSSION POINTS

1. In the first case study, if you had been in Jackie's position, what event objective would you have used?

2. In the first case study there was a need for a session to cover the completion of the checklist paperwork, but what other sessions would you have included to ensure the event achieved its objective?

3. If you had spent a lot of time designing a training event you might be tempted to not review it with the client, in case you had to start again. List all the consequences of a badly designed training event and decide if it's ever worth taking this risk.

```
┌─────────────────────────────────────────────┐
│                                               │
│                      3                        │
│             Planning the Details              │
│                                               │
│                                               │
└─────────────────────────────────────────────┘
```

WORKING ON THE SESSION DETAILS

The design of the training event has now gone as far as a list of working sessions. The next step is to look at these sessions individually and estimate how long each will take. Then the non-working sessions, like refreshment breaks, can be slotted in. Once this is done a complete plan of the event can be drawn up.

Introducing the session sheet
A **session sheet** is a single page on which all the details of the session are recorded (see Figure 7). This can also be done on a personal computer but a print will be needed as the sheets are used at the event by the tutor.

Having copies available
You will need a number of session sheets for each event. Have a session sheet drawn up by a typist or on your personal computer. Then make plenty of copies.

Copying to the session sheet
The information from the session list is copied on to the session sheets starting with session 1, as follows:

(a) session number
(b) event title
(c) title of session
(d) 'to/so that/how' details as they are on session list.

The duration, from and to, are left blank at the moment, as well as the notes and materials.
Then start a fresh session sheet and fill in session 2's details. Repeat this until you have one sheet for each session.
The information shown copied on the session sheet in Figure 7 is from the session list illustrated in Figure 6.

Session __2__   Event HANDLING CUSTOMER COMPLAINTS

Title COMPUTER SYSTEM_____ Duration _____ mins

From ____·____   To ____·____

To/so that:

TO EXPLAIN COMPUTER LOGGING SYSTEM SO THAT

DELEGATES CAN LOG IN COMPLAINTS, SEARCH

FOR INFORMATION AND BACK UP SYSTEM

How:

HANDS ON WITH TERMINALS IN

TRAINING ROOM.

NOTES

MATERIALS

Fig. 7. An example of a session sheet.

WORKING OUT SESSION LENGTH

The duration of each session needs to be estimated, as the first step towards drawing up an overall timetable for the training event.

- Always use minutes. If a session is an hour-and-a-half then write 90 minutes.

- The shortest session is never less than 5 minutes.

- Always work in multiples of 5 minutes: 10, 25, 45, 70. This makes it easier to relate the sessions to the 5-minute division of the clock face.

- When the session duration has been estimated write the time on the session sheet in the space provided.

Knowing the session duration

You may already know how long some sessions will take. Here is an example.

Tourist office staff take winter break to improve image
The manager and the staff of a busy city centre tourist office go to a hotel for two days, to take part in a training event run by the city council training department.

As part of the event there is a session when the group of twelve delegates divides into three groups of four. They are then sent to separate rooms and each group is asked to come up with a list of things that could be improved in the office. The designer has allocated 45 minutes for this session.

This type of session is called a **syndicate exercise**. Syndicate exercises always have a set time period. They can be as short as 20 minutes or as long as several hours. The event designer decides on what he or she thinks is appropriate and no further calculations are required.

Working back from the overall time

If you have been given a fixed time in which to deliver some training you can adjust the length of each session to fit the overall time.

Let's see how this would work for an event at our case study building society.

Building society staff brush up on their housekeeping
The housekeeping training event is to last an hour. Charles draws up a

list of five sessions. There is no complication over refreshment breaks, but there will be a short introduction to explain what the event is all about. Allowing 10 minutes for the introduction, that leaves 50 minutes. So each session can be allocated 10 minutes. In practice some sessions might take longer than 10 minutes, the rest less, but overall the whole event will fit into the time that's been given.

Learning from previous events
A session may have been used before as part of some other event. All you need to do is to look at the file for that event, then you can find the duration of the session. Let's look at an example.

Council road gang learns to be on its guard
A training event is to be run for new recruits to a council road repair department. This is to ensure they are fully aware of the legal requirements for guarding road works. It includes setting out traffic cones, putting up signs and controlling traffic.

One of the sessions takes place outside, with the men setting out cones and signs along an imaginary road chalked out on a playing field. This session has already appeared in many other training events, the most recent being a safety course for managers. It lasts for a whole afternoon, 3 hours, or 180 minutes, in total.

Pinning down a guest speaker
If a guest speaker is being used for one of the sessions the designer must tell them how long the session is. In the following example a guest speaker is brought in because he is an expert in the subject.

Police get on-line to trap phone pests
The chief constable of the county constabulary has nominated an officer at each police station to handle enquiries about nuisance telephone calls. These officers are to attend a one-day training event to familiarise them with the correct procedures.

One of the sessions is to be a talk by a BT manager, to explain how they deal with requests from the police to log and trace calls.

The designer of the training event has contacted the BT manager and they agree to a 45-minute session.

Reading through the script
Some sessions may be covered word for word in a script which will be used by the tutor at the event. The designer can read the session script aloud and time how long it takes, as in the next example.

Railway safety experts arrive on time
A railway company has recently introduced a new style of induction course for staff who have just been taken on. This is a four-day residential event, with a strong emphasis on customer service and safety. The sessions covering safety need to accurately reflect legal requirements. Each of the safety sessions is fully scripted and checked by the company safety manager. The event designer is able to read through the scripts, at the speed he would expect the tutor to work at, to see how long each session will take.

Trying out a dummy run
If a session involves something practical, like building a model or writing a letter on a word processor, this can be tried out by the designer to see how long it takes.

Let's see how running through a session before the event allows an estimation to be made.

Firefighters to play safe in fashion parade
A new-style breathing apparatus is to be issued to all the fire crews in the county fire brigade. Before any of the firefighters are permitted to use this apparatus they must all attend a half-day training event at their regional headquarters, in groups of ten delegates.

One of the sessions involves putting on the breathing apparatus then walking through a simulated smoke-filled room. Each delegate must do this twice.

The length of this session was worked out by the designer of the event by trying out dummy runs. He used five of the regional headquarters staff to try the exercise three times each. From this trial the designer was able to calculate the time the delegates would take to complete the session.

Total time for five staff to do three runs each	$= 90$ minutes
Average time for one person to complete task	$= \dfrac{90}{5 \times 3}$
	$= 6$ minutes
Total time for ten delegates to do two runs	$= 2 \times 10 \times 6$
	$= 120$ minutes

So for the practical session 120 minutes is allocated.

MOVING TOWARDS AN OVERALL PICTURE

Before we look at how to add in the non-working sessions, like refreshment breaks, let's introduce a case study which will help to illustrate how we arrive at the overall event plan.

Admin team's healthy approach to curing problems

This case study is about the Nesscliff Health Authority's admin department, which is to attend a one-day team building event. The event will be run by two tutors: a leader and an assistant. There are twelve delegates.

The work of the admin department is being affected by a number of minor internal squabbles, and by an increase in abusive, and sometimes violent, behaviour by customers who come to the enquiries counter or contact them by telephone.

Event objective

The team of twelve admin department employees will spend one day at the Nesscliff Resort Hotel, to review and resolve the problems which restrict good team working and to learn how to deal with abusive behaviour, and so that the team will work in a more coordinated manner and be able to deal with customers who are abusive or violent.

The case study sessions list

1. Brainstorm internal problems
Brainstorming is a technique to provide a list of items for discussion. This is the starting point for the admin department to address the internal squabbles. (Brainstorming is explained in Chapter 4.) (20 minutes).

2. Syndicate exercise No 1
The brainstorm list has been divided into three smaller lists. These are allocated to three teams of four delegates: teams A, B and C.

The three teams go to separate rooms in the hotel. Their task is to debate the items on their list and decide which is the most important issue. If they could improve on just one item, which one would give the greatest improvement to team working? (30 minutes).

3. Problem solving techniques
Back in the main event room a guest speaker explains how problem solving techniques can be used to get down to the root causes of

difficulties. He then gives some guidance as to how these could be applied to the three problems the syndicate teams have identified. (25 minutes).

4. Syndicate exercise No 2
* Problem A is passed to team B to deal with.
* Problem B is passed to team C to deal with.
* Problem C is passed to team A to deal with.

The teams go back to the syndicate rooms and have 30 minutes to apply the problem solving techniques. They must come up with something positive for the whole department to do, to help eliminate or reduce the problem. While the syndicate exercise is taking place the guest speaker goes round to offer assistance.

The final 15 minutes of this session takes place in the main event room, with the teams reporting back their recommendations. Everyone must pledge to try to adopt these when they get back to the office. (45 minutes).

5. Abusive and violent behaviour
The department's internal problems have been looked at and dealt with. Now the team's attention is on the other issue: how to deal with abusive and violent customer behaviour. For this session a second guest speaker is brought in: a consultant from the psychology department of the local university. She gives a talk and shows a short video. (45 minutes).

6. Role play exercise
A desk is placed in the middle of the room with a chair either side. Each delegate takes it in turn to sit behind the desk, with one of the tutors sitting on the other side and playing the part of an abusive customer.

Each delegate gets 5 minutes of dealing with the imaginary situation. The other delegates look on and the psychologist takes notes. The situations have been worked out in advance and are all different. They have been designed to illustrate the points made in the previous session. (60 minutes).

7. Feedback on performance
The final session is the report back on how each delegate got on in the role play situation. The psychologist gives her opinion, with the other delegates adding their comments. (30 minutes).

STARTING WITH AN INTRODUCTION

All training events should have an opening session or introduction. This sets the scene for the delegates and explains everything they need to know about the place where the event is being run.

A session sheet is also to be used for all non-working sessions like the introduction, but the 'to/so that' and the 'how' statements are not needed.

Figure 8 shows the session sheet filled in for the team building event case study. Let's look at the key features, with some practical suggestions that can be used at your own training events.

Welcoming the delegates

The tutor opens the event by saying a few words of welcome:

'Good morning everyone. Welcome to the Nesscliff Resort Hotel and the admin department's team building event. I'm Simon Scarratt, I'll be leading the event. This is Lynda Leyton, the other tutor, who will be running some of the sessions and generally offering help and support through the day.'

Explaining the domestics

The delegates need to know about the things that will affect their safety and comfort during the day at the hotel. The contents of this part of the introduction will vary according to the type of training event and where it is being held. Here is a list of possibilities.

- what the fire alarm sounds like
- if there will be any fire alarm tests during the event
- location of the fire exits
- where the delegates assemble if the alarm sounds
- location of the ladies and gents toilets
- where delegates are permitted to smoke
- location of restaurant for lunch
- sports facilities for delegates staying overnight
- anything that delegates must pay for themselves
- claiming back expenses
- correct place to park cars
- facilities for private phone calls
- pagers and cell phones to be switched off
- dress requirements for dinner
- any other domestic item delegates wish to ask about.

Session __INTRO__   Event __TEAM BUILDING-ADMIN DEPT__

Title __INTRODUCTION__   Duration __4 5__ mins

From __09:45__   To __10:30__

1. WELCOME THE DELEGATES
2. EXPLAIN THE DOMESTICS
3. TALK ABOUT THE OBJECTIVE
4. INTRODUCE THE AGENDA
5. LAY DOWN THE GROUND RULES
6. FIND OUT WHO'S WHO

NOTES

TEA + COFFEE AVAILABLE FROM 9:30

DELEGATES TO WRITE FIRST NAMES

ON PLACE CARDS.

MATERIALS

COFFEE, TEA + BISCUITS   14 PEOPLE

PLACE CARDS WITH SURNAMES ON

MARKER PENS. AGENDAS. PENS + NOTEPAPER

FOR DELEGATES + TUTORS. GROUND RULES.

PERSONALITY CHECKLISTS

Fig. 8. Introduction to case study event, session sheet.

40

Talking about the event objective

Some of the delegates may be unsure why they are attending the training event. Others may be concerned that they won't be able to cope with all the sessions. The tutor should:

1. Read out the event objective: 'The purpose of this training event is to ... so that ...'.

2. Ask for any concerns with the aims of the event. Examples of typical concerns are:

   (a) Won't be able to keep up with the rest.

   (b) Thinks the event is missing the main problem area.

   (c) Delegate has bad back so he won't be able to lift anything heavy.

The tutor notes any issues raised, and during the event keeps an eye on the people who have raised health or learning issues. Any issues which appear to criticise the aims of the event are dealt with at the closing session.

Introducing the event agenda

As part of the introduction to the event the agenda should be quickly read through by the tutor, to remind the delegates of the sequence of the various sessions. The agenda can be displayed on a flip chart, or a copy given to the delegates.

Laying down the ground rules

Ground rules are necessary to keep the event on track. These can be written on a flip chart or piece of large card, before the event, and presented as part of the introduction, or they can be typed on a single page and handed out to the delegates. An example of a set of ground rules you can use at your event is illustrated in Figure 9.

The expression 'off line' means that any disagreements between delegates and the tutors are discussed over lunch or at other breaks.

Finding out who's who

To get a training event off to a friendly start the tutor should spend some time finding out a few things about the delegates, even if everyone in the room already knows each other.

TRAINING EVENT GROUND RULES

(title and date of event)

- Keep to allocated times.

- Disagreements will be dealt with off line.

- If the tutor is unable to answer a question it will be noted and responded to later.

- Keep to event and session objectives. Don't criticise or try to reorganise the company.

- Don't be critical of the efforts of the other delegates.

Fig. 9. Training event ground rules.

PERSONALITY CHECKLIST

Delegate's name:

Which department do you work in:

How long have you worked for the company:

What other jobs have you done:

What do you expect to get from this training event:

Tell us (use one of the following questions or think of another along the same lines):

- What your hobbies are.
- Something that very few people know about you.
- Three of your likes and three of your dislikes.
- If you have ever met anyone famous.
- About a secret unfulfilled ambition.
- If you were a dog, what kind you would be and why.

Fig. 10. A personality checklist.

The suggested approach is to use a **personality checklist**. A suitable checklist is illustrated in Figure 10. The checklist can be used in two ways:

1. Self appraisal

(a) Allow each delegate 5 minutes to fill in their own checklist.

(b) Go round the room asking each delegate in turn to read from their own checklist, with a maximum of 2 minutes each.

(c) The tutors are also included and need to complete and read out a checklist too.

2. Partners

(a) Delegates pair up, including the tutors.

(b) Give 5 minutes for each person to interview their partner and complete their checklist.

(c) Allow another 5 minutes for the roles to swop over.

(d) Go round the table, asking each person to talk about their partner from the checklist within a 2 minute time limit.

CATERING FOR REFRESHMENT AND LUNCH BREAKS

Write out one session sheet for each refreshment break, and for the lunch break, as follows:

● event name

● title will be either refreshment or lunch

● duration will be 15 minutes for refreshment, 60 minutes for lunch.

Stretching legs during refreshment breaks

The longest time between breaks should be 90 minutes. Having a break every 60 minutes is better. This may mean splitting a long session into two parts to accommodate a break in the middle.

You may have to allow more than 15 minutes if the drinks are not served in the event room and the delegates have to go elsewhere for the break. Or you may think it's a good idea to have extra time for people to go to the toilet, or have a short walk. Too long a break is better than too short.

Event plan for __TEAM BUILDING - ADMIN DEPT__   Page __1__

No	From	To	Session	Duration
—	09:45	10:30	INTRODUCTION	45
1	10:30	10:50	BRAINSTORM	20
—	10:50	11:05	BREAK	15
2	11:05	11:35	SYNDICATE EXERCISE 1.	30
3	11:35	12:00	PROBLEM SOLVING	25
—	12:00	12:15	BREAK	15
4	12:15	13:00	SYNDICATE EXERCISE 2.	45
—	13:00	14:00	LUNCH	60
5	14:00	14:45	ABUSIVE + VIOLENT BEHAVIOUR	45
—	14:45	15:00	BREAK	15
6	15:00	16:00	ROLE PLAY EXERCISE	60
—	16:00	16:15	BREAK	15
7	16:15	16:46	FEEDBACK SESSION	30
—	16:45	17:15	CLOSING SESSION	30

Fig. 11. Case study event plan.

Taking time out for lunch

Always plan for the lunch break to start between 12 o'clock and 1.30 at the latest. The concentration of the delegates is likely to flag if they start to get hungry because lunch is too late.

The duration of the lunch break should always be planned as not less than 60 minutes. If the delegates finish their lunch in 30 minutes the extra time can be useful if the event plan is slipping behind schedule.

Closing the event

The closing session lasts 30 minutes. This includes a review of how well the event went. A full explanation is given in Chapter 9.

LINKING ALL THE SESSIONS TOGETHER

With the session sheets written out for the introduction, refreshment, lunch breaks and the closing session, they can be slotted in amongst the working session sheets.

You will now have the session sheets in the order of the event. An overall plan of the event can be drawn up.

Writing out the event plan

Let's assume the admin department's event starts at 9.45 am. The first session is the introduction which takes 45 minutes. This means session 1, the brainstorm, will start at 10.30. The event plan for the case study is illustrated in Figure 11.

Points to note about event plans are:

• Use 24-hour clock times.

• There are no gaps. The finish time of a session is the start time for the following session.

• Only the working sessions are numbered. These correspond to the numbers on the session list.

Drawing up a plan blank

Have an event plan blank drawn up by a typist, or on your personal computer, and make copies for use at your own training events.

Timing the session sheets

As the event plan is written out, you can now complete the From and To boxes on the session sheets, to show the start and finish times of each session.

Lasting longer than a day

For events that last longer than one day use a separate sheet for each day. You may also have to include evening sessions as part of the plan.

CHECKLIST FOR PLANNING EVENT DETAILS

1. Write out a session sheet for each working session.

   (a) Session number.
   (b) Event name.
   (c) Session title.
   (d) The 'to/so that/how' statements from the session list.

2. Work out the duration of each session. Write the number of minutes on each session sheet.

3. Write out session sheets for non-working sessions.

   (a) Introduction.
   (b) Refreshment breaks.
   (c) Lunch.
   (d) Closing session.
   (e) Include number of minutes in all cases.

4. Put session sheets into order of event. Write in start and finish times of each session.

5. Write out the event plan. List all working and non-working sessions.

CASE STUDIES

Joyce's common sense plan improves Michael's image

Michael knows that his monthly meetings are ineffective and long-winded, and his managers think he's a boring person. So he asks Joyce, one of his managers, to sort out his next meeting for him.

Michael gives Joyce a list of subjects for the meeting agenda. Joyce thinks that many of the items are really training items, where the managers at the meeting will learn something.

Joyce changes Michael's subject list into a training event session list. She writes out individual session sheets, adding an introduction and plenty of breaks. After allocating appropriate durations to each session she produces an event plan.

One of the sessions is about spotting fraudulent cheques. Joyce invites a guest speaker from a local bank, who already has a standard 30 minute presentation on the subject.

The meeting kept to time and everyone thought it was highly effective. Michael agrees future meetings should be run as monthly training updates, with the objective of improving the knowledge, working practices and morale of the team.

Peter's backyard test delivers the goods

Peter, the manager of the three high street video and hi-fi shops, finds his sales have increased. He needs to subcontract the extra deliveries to an additional delivery van owner-driver.

Peter has not previously had to train drivers on handling videos and hi-fi, because they were all experienced. But the new man has not worked with electrical equipment before. To work out the length of the practical handling session, Petter runs a trial at one of his shops. He parks his estate car in the service road. Then he times how long it takes one of his sales assistants to move a selection of equipment from his car then across the yard to the back door of the shop. The backyard is about the length of the average front garden. From the times recorded during the trial run Peter is able to estimate a realistic time for the handling session of his new driver training event.

The training event takes place and the driver is impressed by how well organised it is. The driver sees that Peter needs to be taken seriously if he wishes to be retained as a delivery subcontractor.

Charles ignores the rules and loses his grip

Charles is asked to organise one of the monthly building society area events. These take place after hours and are attended by the staff from the branches within the local area. They cover training issues and informal exchanges of information.

Charles draws up an event plan, but it's a plan without an introduction session and the event has no ground rules.

At the event, during a training session called Being More Customer Friendly, one of the delegates questions why it's necessary for male counter staff to always wear ties. This point has no relevance to the training session, but Charles does not have the benefit of ground rules to bring the event back on track. The discussion develops into a argument over the wisdom of company policy. Nearly an hour is wasted, and there's no time to complete the last session of the event.

The area manager doesn't intervene. She wants to demonstrate to

Charles the kind of difficulty he can get into to if an event does not have a proper introduction session. They discuss this point at their next face-to-face meeting, and Charles agrees he has learnt a lesson and will pay more attention to the event introduction in future.

DISCUSSION POINTS

1. Ground rules can also be used at team meetings and committee meetings. Could you use the same ground rules at these meetings as those for a training event?

2. You have a 120 minute practical session, like the firefighters each taking turns to try out the new breathing apparatus. How can you allow for a 15 minute refreshment break, without stopping the working session in the middle?

3. Using a guest speaker for a session allows you to use their knowledge to cover a specialist subject. What other advantages can you think of?

4
Choosing the Method of Delivery

PRESENTING INFORMATION

For some training event sessions the delegates will simply watch and listen to a presentation. This will be given by the tutor, a guest speaker, or be pre-recorded on a video.

Talking about a subject
Presentations by the tutor or a guest speaker will cover things like:

- how to fill a form in
- the safety regulations associated with an activity
- what to say to a customer when they come in the shop
- how to lay out cones and signs to warn of road works.

Here are some guidelines for talking sessions to make an effective contribution:

- Use visual aids such as flip-charts.

- Always link each talking session to at least one practical session.

- 60 minutes is too long, 45 minutes is the recommended maximum, 30 minutes is ideal.

- Break up long sessions with short interludes of practical items.

- Employ interesting tutors or guest speakers.

Look back at the case study of the Nesscliff Health authority team building event. Session 5 is a 45 minute talk by the psychology expert, but it does include a 15 minute video.

Showing a video
A video presentation at a training event has the following advantages:

- Its duration is known exactly, so it cannot overrun as a guest speaker might.

- It's likely to be of a professional high standard.

- It provides a mental break amongst the other sessions.

- A humorous video can lighten up a boring subject.

Home grown videos
Many large companies have a library of videos within their main training department. Most of these will have been made on the company premises, using professional production teams and a mixture of actors and company employees as extras.

You should ask for a list of what's available, then borrow the ones you think might fit the needs of the training event. View them carefully, and use only if they fit the objective of the session.

Using commercial training videos
Commercial training videos can be bought or hired. They cover a wide range of subjects, and are often available with guide books and other material.

Buying a video with the other material can allow a designer to cover two or three of the sessions of the training event. But designers should go through the descriptions in the catalogues with great care. The theme of a video needs to accurately fit the event objective.

Addresses of video suppliers are given in Useful Addresses.

Three important video don'ts
1. Don't try to make an amateur training video using a domestic camcorder and unskilled actors. The results will be unprofessional and this is certain to spoil the whole event.

2. Don't alter your session objective to fit what's available in the video catalogue. This could adversely affect the overall event objective.

3. Don't use excerpts from movies, or recordings off TV. This is against copyright regulations.

Giving a demonstration
Demonstrations of how to do something are a useful method of giving information to the delegates. For a demonstration to be effective the

following points should apply:

- Delegates can see what's going on.
- Tutor is skilled at giving it.
- Follow up with a 'now you have a go' session.

A typical demonstration would be the tutor showing the delegates from a building society how to fill in a mortgage application form. This could be done on an overhead projector, so that the delegates could see what was going on. A practical follow-up would be the delegates completing sample forms themselves.

ALLOWING THE DELEGATES HANDS-ON EXPERIENCE

Trying things out for themselves is the most effective way for the delegates to learn.

Running dummy computer programs

Dummy programs allow delegates to experience working with a computer before they are let loose on the real thing.

Look back at Chapter 2 and find the Complaints Handling training event session list. Session 2 has the delegates logging trial complaints into the computer. This will be put into a specially written program so that the delegates are not putting rubbish into the main database.

When buying in a new piece of software or computer system you should ask if there's a training package available.

Playing with equipment

If people are being trained to use a particular piece of equipment, you should include a session which allows them to experience its use.

You can also set up simulated situations. For example, delegates being trained to wire houses can work with the equipment fixed to a large board. This is illustrated in Figure 12. All the sockets and light fittings found in a domestic situation are included. The delegate is supplied with cable and tools and he has to wire everything up as if it's a real house.

Important note

All practical sessions involving electrical or mechanical machinery must be preceded by a session covering safety. Any essential safety equipment, such as helmets and gloves, must be available for the delegates.

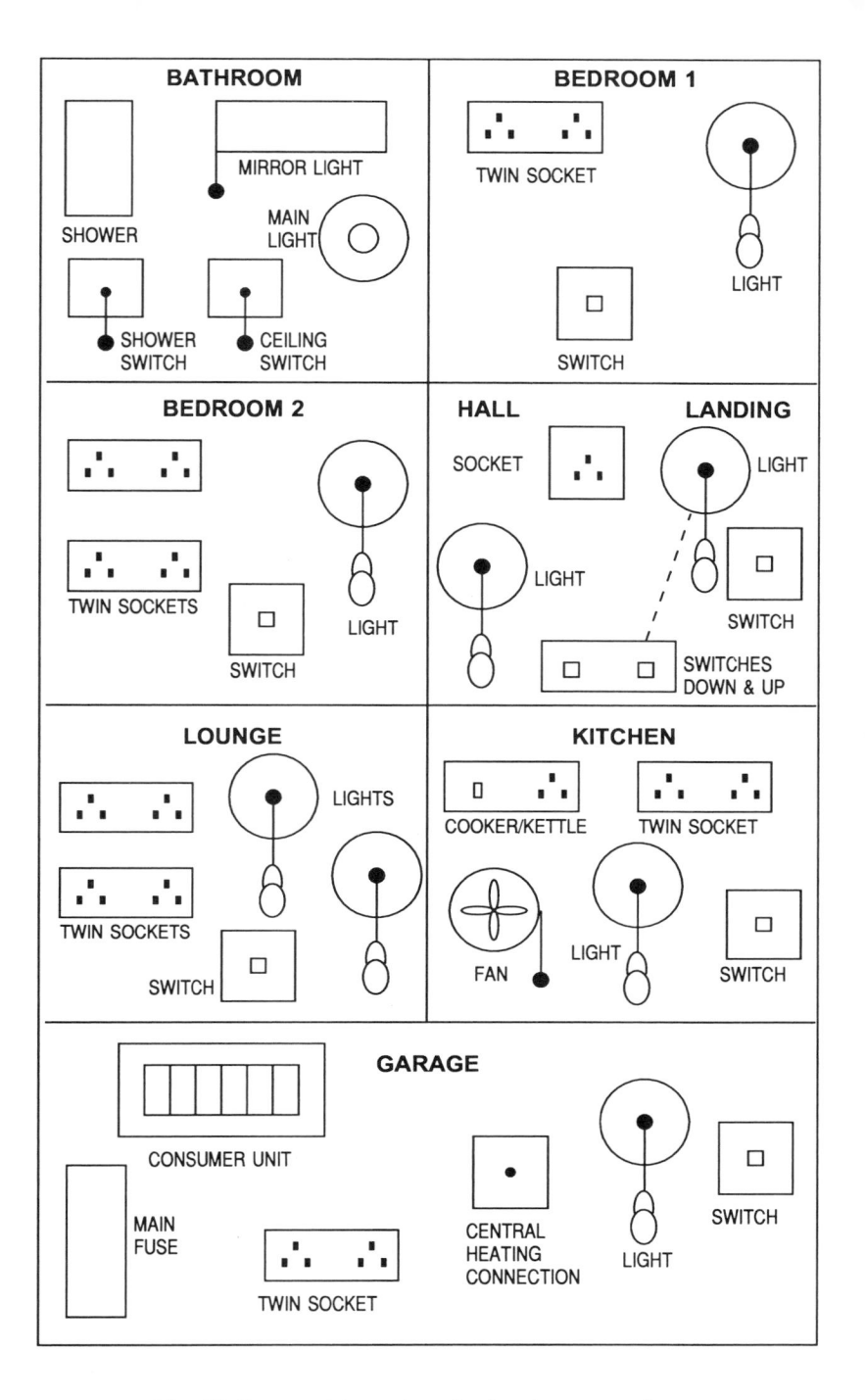

Fig. 12. House wiring set up for hands-on experience.

Answering imaginary enquiries

If you need to give delegates experience in dealing with customer enquiries, a session can be arranged to do this without any contact with real customers. Here's an example.

Arrangement	*What delegate has to do*
Telephone link to delegate from another room. Tutor makes calls and uses examples of normal customer enquiries. Feedback is given of how well orders were taken at end of session.	Answer telephone, deal with enquiries, input information to order forms or computer.

To have a number of delegates working like this at the same time the tutor is assisted by a number of other people making calls. These people can be brought in just for a session. Help can usually be obtained from a company's existing workforce.

Quizzing the delegates

After a presentation, video or demonstration, you can test how much the delegates have learned by using a quiz. The simplest layout is to use a multiple choice question and answer sheet.

● Use three answers per question, with only one correct answer.

● Have a total of ten questions to make the marking and scoring easier.

● Make questions progressively harder.

● You can introduce some humour, particularly in the answers to the first few questions.

An example of a quiz layout is illustrated in Figure 13.

BRAINSTORMING FOR MAJOR ISSUES

You will have seen from many of the case studies that training events are often made up of formal learning, plus more open-ended discussions about problems.

Events designed to deal with the problems facing a team or a

CLIFTON COUNTY CONSTABULARY

Dealing with phone pests   Questions and answers

Delegate's name: Date:

Circle a, b or c, to indicate your choice of answer.

1. When a member of the public first complains about receiving nuisance telephone calls, do you:
    a) Ask if the caller said anything interesting
    b) Tell them to come back if they have any more
    c) Listen sympathetically to what they have to say

2. BT will change a telephone number if:
    a) The customer appears to be in genuine distress
    b) The customer has a letter from the chief constable
    c) The customer pays a £100 fee

    .... and so on, until ...

10. To initiate a call-trace the customer must press digit No 1:
    a) On all types of telephone exchange systems
    b) Only for numbers starting with 0171 and 0181
    c) On most types of electronic telephone exchange

Score 2 points for each correct answer

Score   Rating

18 – 20   Excellent. You have understood our guest speaker.

16 – 17   Good. But you have missed some important points.

10 – 15   Not so good. Perhaps you were asleep while the guest speaker was talking.

0 – 9   Oh dear. Better not apply for that job with BT.

Fig. 13. An example of a quiz layout.

department, and which have a lot of team involvement, are usually called **seminars**. One of the most useful sessions for this type of event is brainstorming. Here's how it's done.

Stating the issue

You need to have a clear, written statement of what the **issue** is. This should be displayed on a flip-chart, whiteboard, or large piece of card. Issues should always start with: what, why, where, when, how or who, for example:

* What are the causes of the low morale in the accounts department?

* Why does the central fire station have the slowest response time on call outs?

Shouting out the answers

Have two tutors if possible, and two flip-chart stands with plenty of paper. Set a time limit of 5 to 10 minutes maximum. Delegates are now invited to shout out anything they feel is relevant to the issue.

− Write all points down even if they are repeats.

− Don't ask for explanations.

− Don't allow a delegate to criticise any point made by another delegate.

− If a point is missed in the confusion, ask the delegate to repeat it.

You may end up with several pages of items. When the time limit expires remove the pages from the flip-chart stand and stick these around the walls of the room.

Incubating the ideas

Give the delegates 10 minutes to look through the list of items. They can get up and walk around the room if they wish. They may also ask for clarification if there's something on the list they don't understand.

Distilling down the list

Here are some examples of the items on the list for the brainstorm of building society customer care issues.

- always say good morning
- more on the counter at lunchtime
- smile at customers
- background music

- no cross-talking
- Charles's awful ties
- flowers on counter
- kid's play corner

There could be as many as fifty items, so you need a method of distilling this down to just a few main issues. Ask the delegates to choose three items each, which would bring about the most significant improvement.

Give the delegates a marker pen each. They write a score on the flip-charts next to the items: 3 for their first choice, 2 for their second choice and 1 for their third choice. The tutor totals up the scores and the item with the highest get the priority for change.

In the example the order was:

- more on the counter at lunchtime

- no cross-talking (counter staff chatting to each other while serving customers)

- smile at customers.

These items can then be dealt with at the next session, or form part of a future training event.

PLAYING VARIOUS ROLES

Role playing is a useful way of directly involving the delegates in a session. This can be done in two different ways:

- The tutor taking the lead role, with the delegates responding to the situation created.

- The delegates being given parts to play, with the tutor looking on and making notes from which feedback can be given.

Setting up a role play

Here is an example where the delegates have been given parts to play. One delegate acts as a customer, the other as a sales person. They are both given written briefs about the roles they are to play.

Playing the customer in a video shop: delegate 1
You have plenty of money to spend, but are reluctant to part with it unless you can be convinced that it's money well spent.

You already have one high quality video at home, but you are thinking of getting a second machine so that you can record two programme simultaneously. You think the cheapest range is your best option.

Being the sales assistant: delegate 2
Your manager would like you to sell the most expensive equipment possible by explaining the advantages of the more sophisticated items over the cheaper versions. You get a larger bonus for selling the expensive items.

Pretending with dummy equipment cards
On the table beside the two delegates are ten pieces of card, each labelled with the name and price of a video recorder.

The delegates are given 10 minutes to act out the situation of the sales assistant trying to sell the customer one of the more expensive video recorders. The tutor looks on, noting how well the sales assistant is using the selling skills learned in the previous session.

After this the delegate is given feedback on how he/she performed. Then the roles of the two delegates are reversed and a new situation is given out on briefing sheets.

CHECKLIST FOR METHODS OF DELIVERY

Use this list as a memory jogger when you're thinking about the methods you will use to deliver the sessions of your training event.

1. Presentations
   (a) talking
   (b) video
   (c) demonstration.

2. Hands-on experience
   (a) computer
   (b) equipment
   (c) customer enquiries
   (d) quiz.

3. Brainstorming
   (a) state issues
   (b) shout out answers
   (c) incubate ideas
   (d) distill down the list.

4. Role playing
   (a) led by tutor
   (b) delegates take parts, tutor observes.

CASE STUDIES

Michael learns a lot from his own mistake

At one of the accounts department's monthly meetings Michael includes a training video called Running Effective Meetings. He hired the video from a commercial training company, choosing it from the description in the catalogue. It uses comedy to get an important message across.

Michael doesn't have time to watch the video before the meeting. As he watches it for the first time, with his managers, he finds out that the main character is very like himself. The video portrays a manager who has very little idea of how to run effective meetings, with everything going hopelessly wrong.

The team thoroughly enjoy watching the video, finding it amusing and informative. And they're even more pleased to hear Michael say he accepts the criticism it makes of people like himself. Michael now tries very hard to make his monthly meetings more productive and effective.

Peter's brainwave solves a shopping mystery

Peter holds a monthly meeting in the back room of a pub, for staff from his three hi-fi and video shops. This meeting is often used for short training items as well as being a social event.

At one of these meetings they have a brainstorming session with the statement: how can we measure our customer image against that of our competitors?

Out of all the ideas listed, one is selected. This is to have mystery shoppers coming into Peter's shops to enquire about goods, services and prices. The mystery shopper will complete an assessment form after he/she leaves. These visits will also be made to the competitor's shops.

Peter uses pupils from the local sixth form college to act as the mystery shoppers, paying them with discount vouchers for his stores. The results of the surveys indicate that some of his own staff need additional training to help them to be more customer-friendly, so he starts having a regular customer service training session at his monthly meetings.

Head office's short-sighted methods leave Geraldine lost

The building society head office has introduced an inter-branch message system linking all the computer terminals. All branches are asked to send one delegate to a half-day training event at head office, to learn how the system works. Charles sends his most efficient customer advisor, Geraldine.

In the training room there is a large screen and a projector linked to the computer system. The tutor demonstrates how to send messages between branches, by sitting at a terminal and showing the delegates what's happening on the large projection screen. This is not followed up by a practical session on the terminals in the room, and the only other information Geraldine is given is an out-of-date handbook.

Geraldine is slightly short-sighted and she wears glasses when she drives her car. She had assumed she would be sitting at a terminal, so she left her glasses in the car. She could not see what was happening on the projection screen in the training room.

On her return to the branch Geraldine is unable to explain anything about the new messaging system. Charles complains to head office about the quality of the training event. Some weeks later a self-teach package is made available, which can be used on the terminals in the branches.

DISCUSSION POINTS

1. Imagine that you have been asked to do a guest speaker session at a training event on your favourite subject. Do you think you could manage to explain it within 45 minutes? And what practical follow-up session would best give the delegates hands-on experience?

2. There are a number of self-teach packages available on computer disk. These are divided up into sessions like any other training event, but the tutor is the software and not a person. What are the advantages and disadvantages of the computer method, compared with the traditional training event?

3. Humorous videos and brainstorming sessions will help to relieve any tension at an event dealing with an important subject. Do you think there's a limit to how much of an event can comprise lighthearted sessions before they become a distraction?

5
Selecting the Right Material

CHOOSING THE RIGHT EQUIPMENT

Some of the equipment you might need at a training event, such as flip-charts, has already been mentioned. Let's now look in detail at how it can be used.

The flip-chart

Flip-charts are pads of A1-size paper which are fixed to an easel. The sheets can be turned over from the top, or torn off individually. A typical flip-chart easel is shown in Figure 14.

A desktop version is also available which takes B1-size pads.

Flip-chart facts
- A presentation consisting of a sequence of points can be listed before the event on a series of pages. The pages are then turned over by the tutor as he/she speaks.

- The tutor can write key points on blank pages as he/she makes a presentation. Then pages are removed or turned over as the tutor moves on to subsequent topics.

- Pages can be pre-printed by a graphics company when high quality presentation material is required.

- Pages with perforations across the top are available when sheets need to be removed cleanly.

- A flip-chart easel gives tutors psychological support. They can keep their hand on it, which stops them waving their arms about, and they can use the items on display as cues for their presentation without having to refer to notes.

- A flip-chart can be used to display a welcome message. For example: Welcome to the Nesscliff Resort Hotel and the admin department's team building event.

- A flip-chart can be used to display ground rules and take down issues during the introduction session of an event.

- You should use large lettering so that people at the back of the room can see. Don't crowd too many points on one page.

- Part of a page can be covered using paper and Blu-tack. It can be uncovered during the presentation.

- The easel legs can be shortened by a series of notches. With the legs completely retracted the easel will stand on a table.

- Paper comes in different thicknesses. If writing shows through from the sheet underneath only write on every other page, or use thicker paper.

- Most training rooms and hotel conference facilities have one or two flip-chart easels as part of the furniture. Check their condition to ensure the mechanism to hold paper at the top is working.

- Don't letter your own flip-charts if you can't write neatly. Find someone who can do it for you.

- Presentations can be made more interesting by adding cartoons or other illustrations among the script. Find someone who is good at these if you're not much of an artist yourself.

Using an overhead projector

The overhead projector shows a magnified image on a screen from transparent slides. The slides can be prepared before the event, or they can be written on as the presentation progresses. Two kinds of overhead projector are shown in Figure 14. The name is usually abbreviated to OHP.

The reflector type is folding and portable, but it is more expensive than the traditional type with the light in the base. An attachment called an LCD panel is available which links to a personal computer, to project the monitor image on the screen. This will only work on the box-type OHP.

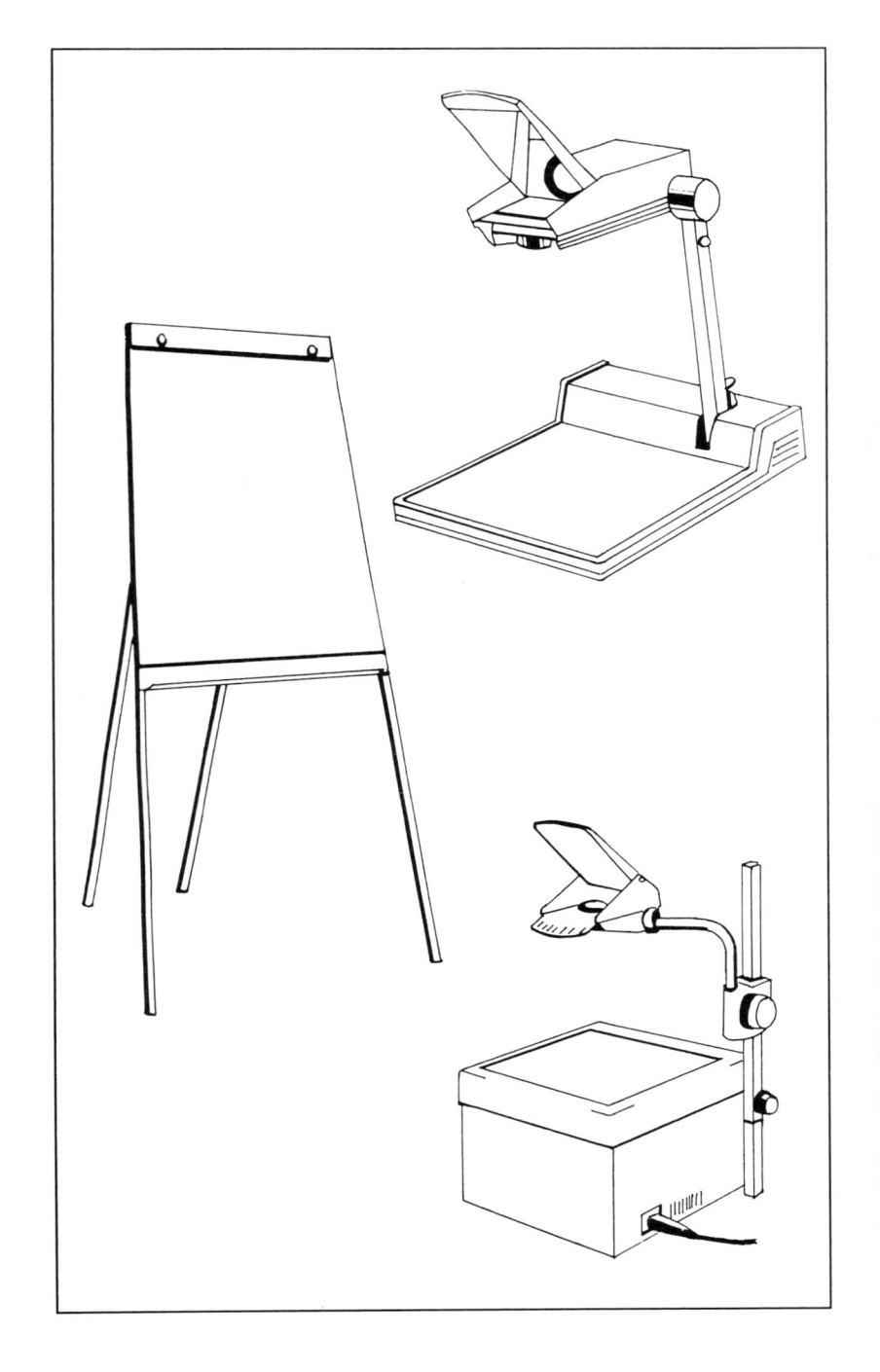

Fig. 14. Flip-chart easel and overhead projectors.

OHP slides are A4-size. They can be written on with pens designed for this purpose. There are alternative types of slide which can be printed on with a photocopier or laser printer.

Paper separators should always be used between unmounted slides to prevent them sticking together. Mounting the slides in card frames makes them much easier to handle.

A training event may use both flip-charts and an OHP. To help you decide which to use here are the advantages and disadvantages of the OHP compared with the flip-chart.

Advantages of the OHP compared with a flip-chart
- Tutor can face delegates while reading from slides.
- Presentation can be done sitting down.
- Slides can be printed directly from a computer.
- Animated graphics are possible with an LCD panel.
- Mounted slides are easy to handle and won't tear.
- The portable OHP can be carried as hand baggage.

Disadvantages of the OHP compared with a flip-chart
- Cost is more than twice as much as a flip-chart easel.
- Room needs to have subdued light.
- There must be a projection screen available.
- Not practical for brainstorming.
- Can't Blu-tack any of the pages to the wall.
- Unmounted slides can stick together.

Most training rooms and hotel conference facilities have OHPs as part of the furniture, but do check it's working and that there is a spare lamp available.

Using whiteboards
A flip-chart stand without a pad of paper can be used as a whiteboard. Most training rooms will also have large, wall-mounted whiteboards.

There are two types: dry-wipe and wet-wipe. It's important to use the correct marker pens. Many of the felt-tip markers that are OK for flip-charts and wet-wipe boards will ruin a dry-wipe board. Whiteboards are useful for:

- recording points raised during brainstorming sessions
- recording issues from delegates to be covered later
- designing training events in the early stages.

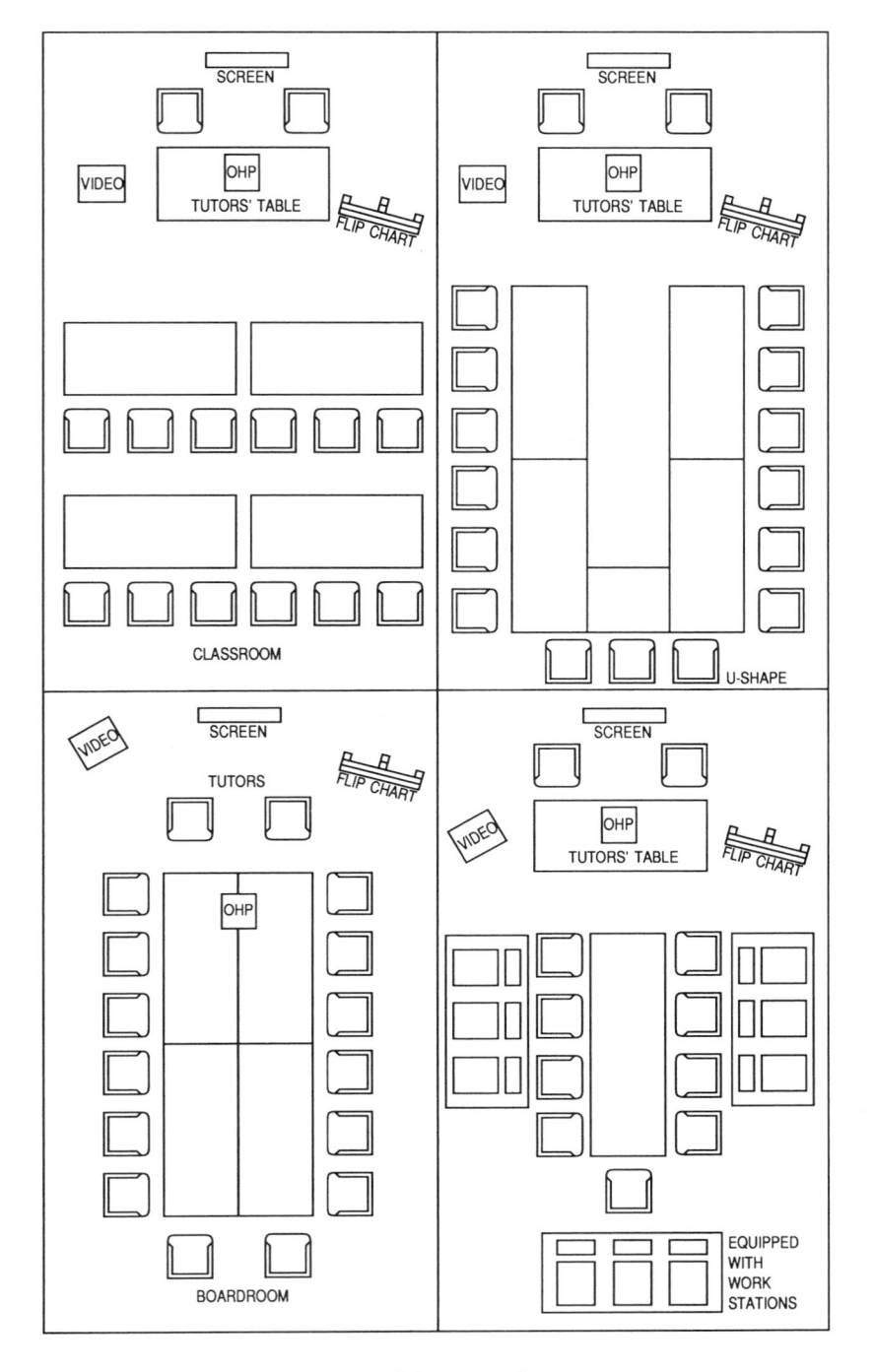

Fig. 15. Training room layouts.

Using video players
Video playing equipment and the associated TV usually come together. Often they are already linked up and sit on a movable stand. Another variation is to have a large screen projection system running off the video player. Here are the advantages and disadvantages of having a video session as part of a training event.

Advantages of a video session
• A wide range of professional material is available.
• Professional material will provide effective learning.
• It will mean less event design work.
• It adds variety to the methods of presentation.
• Can be used to introduce humour.

Disadvantages of a video session
• Equipment can be stolen if not secure.
• Equipment is difficult to transport.
• If equipment is unavailable at the venue, hiring is expensive.
• Video sessions can be a distraction from the event objective if overdone.

As with the other equipment, always check that it's working before the event. Have the video tape in and ready to run from the start.

LAYING OUT THE TRAINING ROOM

For the majority of training events some or all of the sessions will be in a room specially set aside for the event. A room can be set out in different ways; Figure 15 shows four practical plans. Included on these plans are: a screen, OHP, video player and flip-chart easel. The positions indicated are only a general guide to where in the room they might be.

The classroom
In this layout all the delegates face the front and sit in small groups at separate tables.

Advantages of the classroom layout
• Works well for formal teaching situations.
• Suitable for serious subjects.
• Delegates can be divided into teams.

Disadvantages of the classroom layout
- Delegates don't get to know each other.
- People at the back may not be able to see presentations.
- People at the back may be tempted to be inattentive.
- Doesn't create a spirit of belonging to one team.

Example of where this layout would be used
This layout is useful for training people in serious subjects; for example, the police training event on handling nuisance telephone calls.

The U-shape
The delegates face each other around the outside of tables placed together to make a U-shape. In wider rooms more delegates can be accommodated along the bottom line of tables. The tutors can walk up the centre space if they need to talk to a delegate individually.

Advantages of the U-shape layout
- Delegates can see each other.
- Suitable for all general training events.
- Informal and relaxing.
- Tutors can get close to delegates.
- Everyone has equal seeing opportunity.

Disadvantages of the U-shape layout
- Difficult to divide delegates into teams.
- Takes up a lot of floor space.

Example of where this layout would be used
This layout is the most commonly used. It's very effective for training teams of people who normally work together. The Nesscliff Health Authority team building event would use a room layout like this.

The boardroom
In this layout the tables are pushed together and the delegates sit around the outside. The tutors sit at the top end of the table.

Advantages of the boardroom layout
- Suitable for team building events.
- Tutors are part of the team.
- Can be accommodated in smaller rooms.
- Available as standard in many company meeting rooms.

Disadvantages of the boardroom layout
- Can't divide delegates into teams.
- Delegates may feel more important in some seats.
- Delegates on the side at the end may not be able to see the tutors.

Example of where this layout would be used
Using the boardroom layout puts a strong emphasis on everyone belonging to one team. A good place to use this kind of layout would be for our case study building society, at their monthly events. These involve people from all the branches within the district. From day to day they don't see each other very much, but they do all belong to the same company.

Training room equipped with workstations
For training events having computer sessions the ideal arrangement is to have computer workstations on separate tables.

In the example shown the workstations are around the outside of the room, with a boardroom table layout in the centre. The delegates can move easily from practical work on the computers to other sessions at the boardroom table.

The Complaint Handling training event used as an example in Chapter 2 would use a room layout like this.

Important note
The rules governing the siting and use of display screen equipment must be applied in training rooms as well as the normal work place. See the reference section at the end of the book for further information.

Syndicate rooms
In the classroom layout it is possible for people to sit around the individual tables as groups. The only problem is that each group may overhear each other.

Usually, whatever the training room layout, it's better to have other rooms for the delegates to go to for syndicate work. The main event room can be used by one group. So, for example, if the delegates form up into three teams, only two additional rooms are required.

Syndicate rooms are often available as part of a hotel's conference facilities. If the event is being run on company premises, spare training rooms can be used. If none are available it may be possible to arrange to use vacant offices.

Points to remember when planning the use of syndicate rooms:

- They can be smaller than the main room.
- They need a table and sufficient chairs.
- They may need a flip-chart or other equipment.
- Tea and coffee can be a useful addition.

HANDING OUT THE RIGHT INFORMATION

Notes, booklets and other paperwork given to the delegates at a training event are called **handouts**. This material is organised as part of the design of the event, then given to the tutors for use at the event.

Noting the subject details

Notes about the subject being presented can be made available to the delegates as a text or script. For example, at a sales training event for estate agent employees the first session is about developing a caring attitude towards the customer; the notes will explain how this is done and the tutor will also use the text as a guide to what he/she says about the subject.

Summarising the key points

At the end of the notes about a subject it's useful to have a summary of the key points covered. This can be a simple list, or a few short sentences.

Testing the delegates with an exercise

After the summary of key points it's also possible to include a list of questions. Space is provided for the delegate to write their answers down.

After the delegates have completed the exercise the tutor will discuss the answers. Delegates who haven't understood the session, and have put down the wrong information, can then change what they've written.

Working with books

All three of the above items can be combined into a **workbook** as follows:

Session 1
Notes followed by Summary followed by Exercise
Session 2
Notes followed by Summary followed by Exercise

... etc, until all sessions are included.

DEVELOPING A CARING ATTITUDE: SUMMARY	DEVELOPING A CARING ATTITUDE: EXERCISE
• **Listen**: Let customer know you're paying attention. Say 'Yes' or 'I can see that'. • **Repeat**: Helps you understand the customer's needs. Repeat what the customer says in your own words. • **Agree**: Allows the customer to be critical or complain. Say 'You're right' or 'It is difficult'.	Customer says: | Response Everything costs | so much these | days. I don't see | how I can afford | to move house. | | I'd like a small | place just out of | town, but on a | bus route. | | | |

Fig. 16. Workbook summary and exercise.

Caring for the customer

To see how the summary and exercise items link together, let's look at an example which is illustrated in Figure 16.

In the exercise two customer statements are given as examples. In practice there should be at least two more exercise items than the number of key points in the summary. This means that with three key Caring Attitudes in the summary there should be five different customer statements in the exercise.

The summary and exercise will normally face each other on opposite pages of the workbook.

Using ready-made handouts

You can use off-the-shelf documents as handouts, rather than creating them yourself. Examples of these are:

• manuals that come with computers or machines
• government information leaflets
• paperback textbooks
• company booklets and leaflets
• regulatory documents or quality standards

Session __3__   Event <u>NEW WASTE COLLECTION</u>

Title <u>PRACTICAL</u>   Duration <u>120</u> mins

From <u>10:00</u> To <u>12:00</u>

To'so that:

TO ALLOW COLLECTION STAFF TO HAVE HANDS-ON
EXPERIENCE OF LOADING WHEELIE-BINS,
SO THAT THEY WILL BE ABLE TO MANAGE
REAL COLLECTIONS EFFICIENTLY + SAFELY

How:

200 METRES OF DUMMY STREET. 20 WHEELIE
BINS LOADED WITH A VARIETY OF REFUSE.
COLLECTION VEHICLE + EXPERIENCED DRIVER.

NOTES

20 DELEGATES DIVIDED INTO 10 PAIRS,
RUN - THROUGH 10 TIMES.
RELOAD BINS AFTER EACH RUN.
1 RUN SELECTED AT RANDOM TO HAVE 2 BINS
OVERLOADED TO CHECK THAT ARE FULLY AWARE
OF REGULATIONS.

MATERIALS

REFUSE VEHICLE + EXPERIENCED DRIVER.
200 METRE DUMMY STREET — MARKED OUT IN
YARD — CHALK + CONES.
20 WHEELIE BINS. REFUSE IN PLASTIC SACKS —
10 SACKS NEXT TO EACH BIN (200 TOTAL).
2 SACKS TO CONTAIN SOIL + HOUSE BRICKS

Fig. 17. Session sheet with materials listed.

- emergency services advice leaflets
- medical advice leaflets.

Minimising content of handouts

When considering what sort of handouts to use, go for the minimum amount of paperwork which will support the session objective. Ask yourself if the session objective will be achieved if you give the delegates:

- no handouts at all
- role-play exercises which are more effective
- summary of key points
- notes plus summary of key points
- workbook with notes, summary and exercises.

Handing out the handouts

It's important not to have the delegates distracted from a presentation by giving them a handout too early. The recommended points for handing out workbooks and other handouts are:

1. Issue a ring-binder or folder at the event introduction. Handouts are better loose-leaf than bound.

2. Give out relevant pages at:
   (a) The session summary in the case of a workbook.
   (b) The end of a session for other types of handout.

LISTING MATERIAL REQUIREMENTS

Materials required at training events are recorded on the session sheets in the bottom section. The materials needed at a training event include items:

- for both the tutors and delegates
- which guest speakers will require
- which guest speakers will bring with them
- supplied by the owners of the event venue
- as simple as pens and paper-clips
- as sophisticated as computer software.

Wheeling out an example

Let's look at an example of a training event session, to see how the materials section on the session list is filled in. The session sheet is illustrated in Figure 17.

MATERIALS CHECKLIST

Event   Confidence Building   **Date** 25th March 199X
Venue   Main council block
               training room A
Leader/tutor Jackie

Session sheets and event plan   ☐

Coffee/tea 11 people, introduction & 2 breaks   ☐

Agendas for delegates   ☐

Flip-chart stand – already in training room   ☐

Flip-chart pad   ☐

Selection of marker pens   ☐

Pens and note pads for delegates   ☐

Name cards   ☐

Video *It's a Mug's Game*   ☐

Video player and TV – already in training room   ☐

Quiz 10 copies and answer sheet   ☐

O/H projector and spare lamp – already in training room   ☐

Screen – already in training room   ☐

O/H projector slides for presentation   ☐

Role-play cases – 10 example sheets   ☐

Note pad and clipboard for tutor   ☐

Handout booklets   ☐

Event survey questionnaire   ☐

.... ☐

Fig. 18. A materials checklist.

This council is introducing new style wheelie-bins for domestic use. The loaders, who have only ever had experience with standard dustbins, need to be trained to handle the new bins properly. A dummy street is created, with twenty of the new wheelie-bins spread over 200 metres. The twenty delegates work in pairs emptying the bins into a vehicle which is driven along the street. There are ten runs in total. The bins are filled by the tutors, using rubbish from plastic sacks. There needs to be 200 of these to cover all twenty bins and ten runs.

Among the 200 sacks of rubbish are two with bricks and soil in them. These will find their way into two of the bins on one of the runs. This is to see if the men were paying attention during the theory session. Soil and bricks are not allowed in domestic wheelie-bins in this council's area, so the loaders who find these bins should not attempt to empty them into the vehicle. The other loaders will be looking on, so they will learn from this point too.

Drawing up a checklist
So that nothing will be forgotten a checklist of all the materials for the event is written out. This is done by going through each of the session sheets and copying over the details from the materials sections. An example of a checklist is illustrated in Figure 18. Have a materials checklist with blank lines typed up to use for your training events.

PROVIDING AN AGENDA

One of the items on the materials list is an agenda for the delegates. An agenda is a copy of the event plan without the details, such as the duration of each session. An example is illustrated in Figure 19.

You can give the agenda to the delegates by:

• sending a copy to each delegate with the invitation
• handing it out as part of the introduction session
• doing both of these, because some of the delegates may forget to bring the agenda you sent them.

CHECKLIST FOR EVENT MATERIAL

1. Choose the equipment
   (a) flip-chart and easel
   (b) overhead projector and screen
   (c) whiteboard
   (d) video player and TV.

BOROUGH COUNCIL ACCOUNTS DEPARTMENT

Half-day training event: Confidence Building

Wednesday 25th March 199X   Training room A in main block

AGENDA

09.00   Introduction (tea and coffee available from 8.45)
09.45   Video *It's a Mug's Game*
10.00   Fun quiz covering points learned from video
10.30   Refreshment break
10.45   Presentation: Situations at Work
11.15   Role-play exercise
12.15   Refreshment break
12.30   Summing up the role-playing exercise
12.45   Review of training event
13.00   Close

Fig. 19. An event agenda.

2. Select the room layout
   (a) classroom
   (b) U-shape
   (c) boardroom
   (d) equipped with workstations
   (e) added syndicate rooms.

3. Arrange for the most appropriate handouts
   (a) none considered necessary
   (b) role-play instead of paperwork
   (c) ready-mades
   (d) key points summary
   (e) notes and summary
   (f) workbooks.

4. Recording material requirements
   (a) list on appropriate session sheets
   (b) write out a materials checklist for whole event.

5. Draw up an agenda for the delegates. Use the details from the event plan.

CASE STUDIES

Michael's future depends on his department

The local authority accounts department is to get its new computer system, but half the top management team are not convinced this is the right decision. They still think the work should be done by a private company.

Michael realises that if his teams don't meet their performance targets with the new system his department could be closed down.

Michael asks Jackie, a training manager, to design an appropriate training event so that when the new computer system goes on line everyone will be able to use it effectively, with a minimum of errors.

A training room is found with twelve computer workstations around the outside and a boardroom table in the centre. The company supplying the new computer system will make a software training package available. It will also send one of its own tutors to help at the event. Eight consecutive, two-day events are planned, to train nearly ninety people.

Fortunately the training budget has been underspent and the event is able to get underway without delay. All staff are fully trained by the time the new system is installed and working. The initial indications are, after a week with the new system, that the department performance is up to standard.

Peter hands out safety

A female sales assistant from one of Peter's high street stores is shaken but unhurt after some harassment on her way home from work. She needs three days off to recover from the experience.

Half of Peter's staff are female. At one of his monthly back-room meetings he has a special session for the women. He shows them a commercially made video, *Getting Safely Home*, made to alert females to the dangers they are likely to face when travelling alone and the action that can be taken to minimise risks. After the video Peter gives them each a booklet on the same topic which he obtained from his local police station.

This training greatly improves the women's personal safety and reduces the possibility of more sick leave due to harassment incidents.

Using an exercise book helps Charles

Before Charles, the building society branch manager, went on his Managing with Care training event, he dealt with his team members as follows.

Speaking to Geraldine, one of the counter staff, 'You didn't check the video security system while I was out yesterday. The log's not filled in.' Geraldine would reply, 'The equipment blew a fuse. I had to ring for an engineer. You never seem to notice the extra little things we have to do, all you do is criticise.'

The Managing with Care training event used a workbook. The summary at the end of session five said: Never tell a member of your team they've got it wrong. The exercise which followed asked the delegates to write out alternative opening phrases for six given situations.

When Charles returns to the branch the incident now goes like this.

Charles: 'Geraldine, can you help me with a little idea please. I know you will have checked the video equipment while I was away. So I was wondering if you think we need to fill in the log every time? If the equipment is OK, do we really have to note that down?'

Geraldine: 'I couldn't test it yesterday. A fuse had gone. I had to call out an engineer. Perhaps I should have noted that in the log. I do think the log is a good idea. I'll go and write a note in it now.'

DISCUSSION POINTS

1. Imagine you were the tutor at an evening class dealing with the subject running your own small business. Most of the sessions are adequately described in the text of an off-the-shelf paperback. At what point during the ten-week course would you think this book should be mentioned to the delegates? And should you give them a copy as a handout?

2. Looking at the room layouts in Figure 15, what would you estimate as the maximum number of delegates possible in each case? With too many delegates those at the back may not be able to hear or see properly. Which layout would allow for the most delegates?

3. The tutor can remain seated while making a presentation with an OHP. Why do you think it's usually better to talk to the delegates while sitting down? And can you think of any disadvantages there might be?

6
Finding the Best Places

DEALING WITH TRAVELLING TIME

This chapter looks at training event venues, and the accommodation needed if the event is to last longer than one day.

Getting off to a good start

To get a training event off to a good start everyone needs to be there at the starting time and the delegates must not be travel-weary. Here are some guidelines:

1. If the venue is at the delegates' usual place of work, their normal start times can be used.

2. For other venues three hours should be the maximum travelling time by any method of transport. A 10 o'clock start is recommended.

3. If travelling is to be longer than three hours the start time should be at 1 o'lock, after you have provided the delegates with a decent lunch.

4. An overnight stay the night before can be used to achieve a 9 o'clock start on day one.

5. Don't guess travelling times. Ask someone who regularly makes that journey. If it's by car then allow extra time for traffic delays.

6. Always provide refreshments for the delegates on arrival, and have this available at least 15 minutes before the event start time.

7. When the delegates are required to stay overnight the tutors should stay at the same place, even if they live locally.

PICKING THE RIGHT VENUE

Let's look at suitable venues. Accommodation for overnight stays is covered in the next section.

Using training rooms on company premises

Many large companies have rooms set aside for training purposes. Smaller organisations may also have a room allocated solely for training purposes, if it can be justified on the basis of regular use.

Advantages of training rooms on company premises
- Designer does not have to search for a suitable venue.
- Hire cost can be zero, or a nominal transfer charge.
- Should be fully equipped with flip-charts, etc.
- Likely to meet all health and safety requirements.
- Delegates do not have to travel.
- Delegates will not have to stay away overnight.
- Catering may be available from company restaurant.

Disadvantages of training rooms on company premises
- Sometimes difficult to book your preferred times.
- Interruptions possible from people you work with.
- Equipment can be in a poor state due to over-use.
- Delegates may feel they're still at work.
- Rooms sometimes taken for storage space or offices.
- Syndicate rooms not always available.

Searching out other rooms on company premises

Other rooms can sometimes be found on company premises, which can be used for training purposes. For example:

- boardrooms and meeting rooms
- vacant offices, or manager away on holiday
- rest room, at a time when no one else needs it
- unused area in workshop or open-plan office
- offices out of normal working hours.

Advantages of using other rooms on company premises
- Often available at no cost.
- Delegates do not have to travel.
- Will solve problem of nothing readily available.

Disadvantages of using other rooms on company premises
- Interruptions possible.
- Might not meet health and safety requirements.
- Could give impression of doing things on the cheap.
- Essential equipment may not be available.
- Delegates may have to attend out of hours.

Going to company training centres

Many large national companies have training centres to which the various branches and offices can send delegates. These centres may also offer training event design services and professional tutors. Accommodation blocks are usually available for overnight stays.

Advantages of going to company training centres
- Will be fully equipped to a high standard.
- Catering, housekeeping, organisation all done for you.
- Fixed range of costs and settlement of bills.
- No difficulty with finding overnight accommodation.
- Location maps and other information available.
- Standard of catering and accommodation known.
- Less chance of interruptions.
- Possibility of meeting people from other offices.
- Will meet health and safety requirements.

Disadvantages of going to company training centres
- Delegates may feel they are still at work.
- Centre's tutors may not do things your way.
- May be difficult to book in when you want to.
- Can be a long way from some offices.
- They can lack atmosphere and can be boring places.

Opting for hotel conference facilities

Many hotels have rooms set aside equipped with flip-charts and OHPs for training events. Other rooms will be available as syndicate rooms. They may also offer fax, photocopying and other office services.

Advantages of using hotel conference facilities
- Delegates away from work on neutral ground.
- Overnight accommodation available on site.
- Free of interruptions.
- Atmosphere can be comfortable and relaxed.
- Venue can be near to delegates' place of work.

- Sports and other recreational facilities available.
- Informal meetings in the bar at night.

Disadvantages of using hotel conference facilities
- Can be expensive.
- Standard of service unknown unless previously tried.
- Delegates may not sleep well in strange beds.

Guidance on the use of evening sessions
With the training event and accommodation at the same place, it is possible to have sessions in the evening. Here are some points which will help you decide if you should have sessions in the evening. Evening sessions should only be run if:

1. They contribute to the overall event objective.
2. They are a necessary part of the event plan.
3. You are sure the delegates will not be too tired.

Considering alternative event venues
These are the most commonly used venues for training events, but there are others, such as:

- local authority town halls and meeting rooms
- parish halls and church committee rooms
- schools and colleges outside term time
- large privately owned houses
- craft centres, museums and art galleries
- holiday centres off-season
- back rooms in public houses.

Advantages of using an alternative venue
- May be cheaper than hotel conference rates.
- Unusual locations can increase delegates' enthusiasm.
- No interruptions by normal business enquiries.
- There may be situations to learn from at the location.

Disadvantages of using an alternative venue
- Materials such as flip-charts may not be available.
- Accommodation may not be on site.
- Possibility of too many external distractions.
- Uncertainty over warmth, lighting, catering, etc.

Finding an alternative venue is more difficult than opting for a hotel with conference facilities, or a training room within your own organisation. Start by telephoning possible places and ask if they have a room (or rooms) that can be hired for training events. If you get a positive response your next step should be to see what facilities are on offer, and to get some prices and other details in writing. Be prepared to be helpful with details such as room layouts if they have not had an event there before.

Splitting event venue and accommodation

Another possibility is to have the event venue at one site and accommodation somewhere else. This arrangement can work well. The main advantage is that the delegates don't get the feeling of being shut up in one place for several days, but consider the following points before trying this arrangement.

• Can the delegates travel between the two places?

• The maximum travelling time should be 30 minutes.

• Sorting out the arrangements is double the effort.

• The style of the two places should be matched.

The last point means that if the event is being run in a 12th-century barn at a local folk museum, the hotel should not be a modern concrete and glass building.

The objective of a training event is more likely to be met if the delegates are happy with their surroundings.

MAKING THE VENUE ARRANGEMENTS

This section refers only to the training event venue. If the event is being held in a hotel, and the delegates are staying overnight, then add in the accommodation items from the next section.

Having a look for yourself

If you have the responsibility of designing a training event you should look at the event venue yourself before making any booking. Don't rely on written information or verbal statements of what's available. Even if you have been there before things can change in just a few months, so go back and have another look.

CHECKLIST FOR TRAINING EVENT VENUE ITEMS

1. Sufficient space for delegates and tutors ☐
2. Number and size of syndicate rooms adequate ☐
3. Sufficient tables and chairs ☐
4. Furniture and room allows planned layout ☐
5. Hire charges available in writing ☐
6. Dates required are free ☐
7. Right materials available on site ☐
8. Equipment works, including curtains and blinds ☐
9. Heat, light and ventilation up to standard ☐
10. Room layout responsibility ....
11. Site manager given a copy of layout if he/she needs it ☐
12. Refreshments/lunch responsibility ....
13. Site manager given a copy of agenda showing breaks ☐
14. Fire alarms and escape routes ☐
15. Supply and placing of direction signs ☐
16. Early delivery of event material possible ☐
17. Car parking arrangements satisfactory ☐
18. Direction maps available ☐
19. Descriptive leaflets available ☐
20. Male and female toilets clean and adequate ☐
21. Restaurant for lunch satisfactory & menu available ☐
22. Hire fees inclusive of VAT etc ☐
23. *Review event design and arrangements with client* ☐
24. All requirements confirmed and fees agreed ☐
25. Revisit site before start of event ☐

Fig. 20. Checklist for event venue.

Don't assume that hire charges will remain the same either. This is particularly important for people running courses to make money. If you continue to offer your courses at the same fees, and the hire charges unexpectedly rise, your profits will reduce accordingly.

Checking out the event venue

A checklist of items you should consider when booking or hiring a training event venue is given in Figure 20. This includes arrangements you may have to make with the site management, such as delivering the event materials in advance of the start of the event, and who is responsible for laying out the room. You should also ask for maps and leaflets which you can give to the delegates.

Item 23, checking arrangements with the client before making a final commitment, is explained later in this chapter.

BOOKING INTO ACCOMMODATION

If the training event lasts for more than one day accommodation for the delegates will need to be arranged.

Judging the standard of accommodation

You can use the following points as a guide to the accommodation on offer:

- hotel star or other rating
- brochure
- price list
- recommendations.

There is, though, no substitute for having a look yourself. Ask to be shown round. If they really want your business they will be happy to show you their rooms and other facilities.

Checking out the accommodation

A checklist of items you should consider when looking for suitable accommodation is given in Figure 21.

Hotel chains often have special discount arrangements with companies, or there may be a discount for block bookings; so it is important to ask. Remember to discuss all the arrangements with the client before making the booking.

If the accommodation is the same place as the event venue, the accommodation checklist should be added to the venue checklist and both used at the same time.

CHECKLIST FOR TRAINING EVENT ACCOMMODATION ITEMS

1. Style and atmosphere match event venue ☐

2. Sufficient rooms for delegates and tutors ☐

3. Available for event dates ☐

4. Tariffs inclusive of VAT etc ☐

5. Discount available for block booking/company name ☐

6. Special diets catered for and menu available ☐

7. Agree time for dinner ☐

8. Breakfast times fit in with event plan ☐

9. Tea making, TV and other facilities in rooms ☐

10. Standard of rooms, restaurant and bar satisfactory ☐

11. Facilities available for private phone calls ☐

12. Swimming and other sporting facilities available ☐

13. Direction maps available ☐

14. Brochure or leaflet available ☐

15. Clarify method of payment and who settles ☐

16. *Review event design and accommodation with client* ☐

17. Make booking and obtain written confirmation ☐

18. Revisit a few days before event ☐

Fig. 21. Checklist for delegate and tutor accommodation.

ORGANISING YOUR FILE

The design of the training event has reached an important stage, but you need to review the arrangements with the client before finalising the bookings and inviting the delegates. Let's look at what you'll have in your file of information to take to the client.

Using a standard contents list

A standard title and contents page for the designer's file is illustrated in Figure 22. Have this page typed up with the titles blank, to use with the file of your training event. Note the following two points:

Code

This is a number to identify the training event. It's necessary if your company runs a number of different events through the year with similar titles.

Proposed dates

The proposed dates are when the event is scheduled to take place. In the example this event will be run twice.

MINEFIELD ESTATE AGENTS PLC   **Event designer's file**

Title: Sales training   **Code**: MEA132/98

Proposed dates: 21 − 24 March 199X   7 − 10 June 199X

Contents:
1. Client's requirements
2. Event objective
3. Session list
4. Event plan and session sheets
5. Materials inc. room layout and checklist
6. Venue and accommodation details
7. Final review: notes
8. Delegate list, invitations and replies
9. Measurement of event success
10. Appendix of tutor material

Fig. 22. Designer's file: title page and contents.

Looking at the file organisation

So far this book has only got as far as section 6. The remaining sections are listed to show what the complete file will be like after the event has been run. Always try to use this layout, even for simple training events. Good organisation is the key to effective training.

Using a ring-binder

Use a ring-binder with numbered dividers to correspond to the file sections. The event title and contents page will be in front of the first divider. For short, simple events, dividers are not necessary, but number the papers to this contents list. Include all relevant papers in each section. For example, section 6 will contain checklists, correspondence, receipts, in fact anything to do with the venue and accommodation.

Tutor material

Section 10 is an appendix of tutor material. This is the master copies of handouts, workbooks, etc. If these can't be fitted into the file they are held separately and section 10 will contain a note of where they are kept.

CARRYING OUT THE FINAL REVIEW

You should go back to the client with the details of your event design, prior to making a firm commitment to the booking of the venue or accommodation.

It's unlikely that at this stage you will have to make major changes. You have already carried out a review to agree the event objectives with the client. Take notes during your meeting with the client. If possible you should also ask the client to sign to say that he or she accepts that the design meets the client requirements.

If there is no client, ask someone else to help you with the review.

Even if the event is short and simple it's still good practice to go through all the paperwork prior to finalising the arrangements. File all the review notes in section 7 of the designer's file.

CHECKLIST FOR FINDING THE BEST PLACE

1. Allow for travelling time. Set starting time accordingly.

2. Select event venue.
   (a) purpose-built training rooms
   (b) other rooms on company premises
   (c) company training centres

(d) hotel conference facilities
(e) alternative venues.

3. View the event venue. Use the checklist as a guide.

4. Select and view delegate and tutor accommodation. Use the checklist as a guide.

5. Ensure all event information is filed. Use standard title page and contents list.

6. Make final review with client.
   (a) agree and sign off
   (b) file all notes.

7. Go ahead with venue and accommodation booking.

CASE STUDIES

A step back in time

The local authority accounts department has been using its new computer system for six months. Everything is running smoothly and all performance targets are being met. There is no longer a threat of closure but the department head, Michael, has been told he must reduce his overall expenditure. Two of the team managers agree to take early retirement. This will help meet the new budget targets, but the remaining managers must take on larger teams.

Michael identifies the need for some additional training to help the managers cope. He suggests a two-day event away from the office, to be a mixture of team building exercises and formal skills training. He asks Joyce, one of his team managers, to find a suitable venue and accommodation. Meanwhile Jackie, the training manager, will design the content.

Joyce knows a family who run a craft business at a 13th-century manor house. Their large dining room is sometimes used for meetings. There's a restaurant on site and coffee can be made available.

There's no flip-chart easel or OHP, but these can be borrowed from the local authority training centre.

Joyce arranges overnight accommodation at a hotel four miles from the venue, in an old fishing village with a reputation for being haunted by the ghosts of smugglers.

The event is a great success, helped by the unusual and interesting surroundings. The managers return to work keen to implement the new skills they have learnt, and to work as a more effective team.

A room of their own

Peter has been using the back room of a local pub for his monthly meetings, but some of his staff are unhappy about attending events at this venue.

He decides to convert an old garage into a training room. The garage is at the rear of one of his high street hi-fi and video shops. Some of his staff volunteer to come in on a Sunday to clear the garage out. Peter provides an old carpet and a couple of trestle tables which he covers with a large cloth. He buys twenty secondhand office chairs, which he puts round the two tables in a boardroom arrangement, and a flip-chart easel and an OHP.

The walls are painted and a portable gas heater an electric kettle installed. Peter can now have a proper training programme because all his staff are keen to attend his monthly events in their new training room.

Dull hotel does not cater for Geraldine's taste

Geraldine is sent to a three-day customer care training event run by the building society regional training unit. It takes place in a low-budget motel next to a busy motorway junction. The motel specialises in providing low-budget conference facilities.

On her return Charles, the branch manager, asks Geraldine what she thought of the course. Geraldine tells him she didn't learn very much; accommodation problems distracted her from the event objective. The shower in her room didn't work; she had difficulty sleeping because of the noise of the traffic; the restaurant was unable to provide her with vegetarian meals and the general atmosphere of the venue was dull.

DISCUSSION POINTS

1. The two tutors live near to the hotel where the delegates are attending a three-day sales training event. Budget restrictions do not allow the tutors to stay at the hotel overnight with the delegates. What could the tutors do to avoid the delegates feeling the tutors are not part of the team?

2. Imagine you are the manager of a hotel with conference facilities. You think a publicity pack of information would be useful to give to people looking for a training event venue. What items would you include in this pack?

3. If you were organising a week-long training event at a hotel you would probably choose one with sports facilities for the delegates. Can you think of any other features that could be offered to help the delegates feel more relaxed at the event?

7
Inviting the Delegates

INCLUDING THE ESSENTIALS

This chapter looks at how delegates are invited to a training event.

Inviting the delegates by letter
It is important for the delegate to know everything about the event they're being invited to attend. Delegates will be more at ease if all the uncertainties are dealt with by providing enough information in the invitation. These items may have to be included:

- event title, date and venue
- the event objective
- start and finish times
- an agenda
- how to get to the venue and/or hotel
- booking in arrangements
- details of accommodation and arrangements for paying
- items delegate needs to bring to the event
- looking forward to meeting you
- ask for confirmation of attendance
- ask if they have any special needs or concerns.

Inviting members of the team
The invitation letter illustrated in Figure 23 uses the case study from the last chapter of the two-day team building event for managers from the local authority accounts department.

Because the invitation is from one manager on the team to another, an internal memo has been used. The invitation is to a delegate who is coming by train. Some of the other delegates are using their own cars, so their letters will be different.

INTERNAL MEMO

To: Sandra Scott   **From:** Joyce Defries

Dear Sandra

Team Building Event – May 4–5th 199X – Overton Hall

You are invited to attend our two-day team building event at Overton Hall. The event has been designed by our training manager Jackie, who will also be our tutor over the two days. The objectives are:

1. To develop our existing management skills so that we are all able to run larger teams.
2. To take part in team exercises so that the accounts unit can work even more effectively as one team.

The event starts at 10am on the first day, with coffee available from 9.30am, and finishes at 4.30pm on day two. An agenda is enclosed.

As you have a preference for travelling to and from the event by train, I have checked the times and suggest the following arrangements:

08.47 from Baschurch   16.50 from Overton
09.23 arrive at Overton   17.26 arrive Baschurch

I have booked a taxi to take you to and from the station. This will cost £4.50 each way. Please pay the driver and claim back the cost, together with your rail fare, through the company travel account.

On arrival at Overton Hall, use the entrance by the restaurant and follow the signs to the Tower Studio on the first floor. I enclose a brochure from the Hall.

At the end of day one we shall go to Morgan Harbour Village. David McBride will give you a lift there and back. A room has been reserved for you at the Captain Morgan Hotel. Dinner is booked for 7.30, and it is hoped that we shall all meet for an informal get-together in the bar at 7.

The cost for bed, breakfast and dinner, including VAT is £87. Can you please settle this in the morning before we return to the Hall, and claim it back through the company travel account. The hotel accepts all major credit cards.

All the delegates will be asked to make a short presentation about themselves at the start of the event. Please see the enclosed set of ground rules which give guidance on what preparation is required.

Finally I am looking forward to meeting everyone at the event, which I am sure you will find interesting and enjoyable. Please confirm that you will be attending, and let me know if you have any special dietary needs or any concerns.

Yours sincerely

Joyce Defries

Fig. 23. An invitation letter.

INVITING EXTERNAL DELEGATES

If you are running training events on a commercial basis the delegates will be coming from outside your own company. This will apply when:

• You are running training events as a business, to make money.

• Your company is offering its skills and knowledge to outsiders, to make money or to support the sale of its products.

Asking for payment
For commercially run training events, don't offer places to people who promise to pay; only give places to people who pay *in advance*.

Advertising commercial events
A practical approach is to have an invitation in the form of a printed leaflet. This includes information about the event and a booking or registration form.

An example of a leaflet for a presentation skills one-day seminar is illustrated in Figure 24. This event is being put on by a supplier of visual aids material.

• The leaflet is double-sided and folded across the middle. You can also have leaflets with two or three folds.

• The registration form should be on the back of the title section so that when it's returned important information for the delegate isn't lost.

• Location maps and venue details can be included on the leaflet or sent with a confirmation letter.

• These leaflets don't have to be on glossy paper. A small business can use a personal computer and photocopier.

CONFIRMING THE BOOKINGS

When a delegate agrees to attend a training event you should confirm that a place has been reserved.

• Include additional information not already given in the invitation, for example directions to the venue.

OUTSIDE

AGENDA

08.30 Reception and registration
09.15 Introduction
10.45 Coffee break
11.15 Vocal techniques
12.00 Break for questions
12.50 Lunch
14.00 Visual aids
15.30 Question time, and trying out visual aids
16.00 Tea and close, and chance to talk to tutors

INSIDE

PRESENTATION SKILLS

One Day Seminar on How to be a More Powerful and Confident Presenter

A high value, low cost seminar on the key aspects of presentation skills, so that the delegates will be able to:

◆ adopt techniques to motivate and inspire an audience

◆ use their voices to reach the back row without effort

◆ deliver with style and effectiveness

◆ use the correct visual aids to enhance presentations

Free lunch ◆ refreshments ◆ notes ◆ presentation guide

REGISTRATION AND BOOKING FORM

£106 inc VAT per delegate   Name ....

Address ....

Post Code............ Phone............ Fax............

☐ Baschurch University 14th May
☐ Overton Hall 21st May
☐ Nesscliff Resort Hotel 17th June

Method of payment   No of delegates.......

☐ Cheque no .... £................

☐ Amex ☐ Access ☐ Mastercard ☐ Visa no ....

Signature................ Date ....

Post or Fax to: Garden Studio Training, Baschurch, LI98 772.

Fax: 07763 660055

Fig. 24. An invitation leaflet.

● When delegates are required to pay for a place at a training event, include a thank you for the payment as part of the confirmation.

● The confirmation can be in the form of a printed card which the delegate is asked to produce on arrival. If proof of identity is also required for security reasons, specify what to bring as part of the confirmation, eg driving licence.

DIRECTING DELEGATES TO THE RIGHT PLACE

In our case study of the team building event at Overton Hall some of the delegates will be arriving by car. At the end of day one all the delegates and the tutor will travel to a nearby hotel. The delegates will need maps, and notices will be necessary at the venue because it is a large, rambling building.

Mapping out the route

The recommended style for a map and directions is illustrated in Figure 25.

- If the venue or hotel can give you a copy of a map already drawn up, then use that.

- Simplify roads to straight lines and omit details. Don't worry about scale being correct.

- Black and white photocopies of road maps or street plans are not recommended.

- Start your map from the point at which the driver will leave a motorway or a trunk road.

- Include landmarks just before changes of direction, such as telephone kiosks, railway bridges that cross over the road, and filling stations.

- In addition to the map have a few lines of written directions the driver can memorise.

- Check the route yourself before issuing the maps.

- Include the telephone number of the venue and/or hotel, so that a delayed driver can make contact.

DIRECTIONS

Motorway to Overton Hall

Leave M99 at junction 23. Take B9932 which is signposted with a brown heritage sign to Overton Hall. After three miles, along a winding country road, you'll come to a telephone kiosk on the left. Entrance to Overton Hall is 100 yds further on.

Overton Hall to Captain Morgan Hotel

Turn left at end of drive. Keep on B9932. After 4 miles you'll pass Overton railway station and go under a railway bridge. Half a mile further on bear left at the junction then take first exit from next roundabout. Follow the A900 which is signposted to Cliffville. After one mile turn left on to the A999, then take the next right (100 yds). Go down the hill to the bottom, then follow road around a sharp left-hand bend. Hotel is about 500 yards along the harbour front.

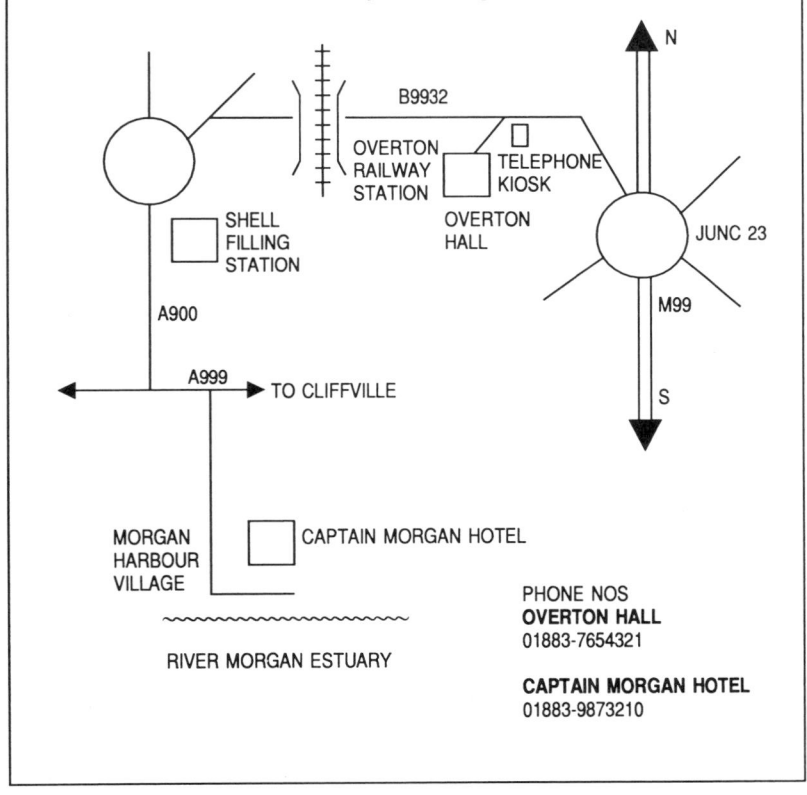

Fig. 25. Map and directions for case study event.

Showing delegates the way

For some training events the invitation letter will tell delegates to report to a reception point. The people on reception can then direct the delegates to the correct room.

For other events you will need to provide sign-posts, or ask the venue management to do this for you. Effective sign-posting will ensure delegates get to the right room and arrive on time for the start of the event. Examples of direction signs are illustrated in Figure 26.

Fig. 26. Examples of direction signs.

DELEGATE LIST

EVENT PRESENTATION SKILLS   DATE 14TH MAY

NO. PS2/98   LOCATION BASCHURCH UNIVERSITY

NO.	NAME	ADDRESS	PHONE NO.	NOTES	✓
1	PETER HINDE	3 THE NOOK BASCHURCH BA3 77Q	0367 543298	PAYMENT RCVD BOOKING CONFD	
2	SALLY GRIMES	24 THE CRESCENT MIDDLETON MD7 35Z	0339 664281	PAYMENT RCVD BOOKING CONFD MAY SWOP TO 21 MAY AT OVERTON HALL	
3	JULIA D'ARCY	261 PENWELL RD YARDWELL YL4 55Y	0289 372199	PAYMENT RCVD BOOKING CONFD VEGETARIAN FOOD ONLY	
4	JOHN LINE	IVY COTTAGE PEARHAM NR. COTTSVILLE CT9 3JT	0897 352 281	PAYMENT RCVD BOOKING CONFD	
5	LIZZIE BARR	61 ARNDALE DR NESCOTT ND8 58T	0296 565665	PAYMENT NOT SENT WITH APPLICATION PHONED LIZZIE 10TH APRIL	

Fig. 27. An example of a delegate list.

96

Choosing a taxi company

If you need to arrange for a taxi to pick up delegates from a railway station or airport you will want to choose a reliable company. Reliability is more important than cost. Your training event could be seriously disrupted if delegates are late arriving because a taxi did not turn up on time. Choose a firm that:

- provides an airport service because they will be experienced in good time-keeping
- will find your delegate by holding up a card displaying the delegate's name or company
- will agree a price in advance.

If the booking is made several weeks in advance of the event you should confirm the arrangements a day or two prior to the event.

LISTING THE DELEGATES

You will need to make a list of the delegates who are to attend your training event. The list for delegates from within your own company will be organised differently from a list of external delegates.

Listing internal delegates

For a training event run within a company for its own people, the delegate list will work out as follows.

- It is a list of names and departments.
- List becomes firm after delegates agree to attend.
- Formal invitations are sent to each delegate on list.
- List is finalised as formal acceptance is received.
- List is available at event to check everyone is there.

Listing external delegates

For companies running training events on a commercial basis a delegate list needs to have additional information. An example is illustrated in Figure 27. Delegate addresses are needed because:

- You will need to send confirmation of a place being reserved.
- You may need to contact them urgently due to a last minute change.
- It will act as a mailing list for future event advertising.

The last column is to use at the event, to tick against who is there. If a delegate fails to turn up they may have forgotten to come, or there may be a crisis at home. Normally you should stick with the agreed cancellation rules, but if the delegate does appear to have had genuine difficulties beyond their control a refund may be appropriate. Alternatively you may be able to offer them a place on another similar event.

Important note
Always use handwritten delegate lists unless you have registered with the Data Protection Registrar. You risk an unlimited fine if you record personal details on a computer without being registered, even for something as simple as names and addresses.

CHECKLIST FOR INVITING DELEGATES

1. Inviting internal delegates
   (a) do it in writing
   (b) include all relevant information
   (c) ask for confirmation of attendance
   (d) ask for any special needs.

2. Inviting external delegates
   (a) combine with advertisement
   (b) include registration form
   (c) always take payment in advance.

3. Confirm a place has been reserved
   (a) include other information such as maps
   (b) book taxis.

4. Draw up a delegate list. Include addresses for external delegates.

CASE STUDIES

Sandra's concerns are allayed
Sandra Scott is one of the team managers in the local authority accounts department. She has been invited to attend the two-day team event at Overton Hall.

Sandra is a good team manager, but fairly nervous and unsure of herself away from the office. Joyce, who has made the arrangements for the event venue and accommodation, has given a lot of details in the invitation. Sandra finds this very reassuring.

A taxi has been arranged to collect her from the station. On the day the driver is waiting on the platform, holding up a card with Sandra's name on it. She had been worried about getting to Overton Hall. The station is several miles away and she had not been very confident that the taxi would be waiting for her. Sandra thoroughly enjoys the training event.

Garage meetings boost Peter's sales

Peter now has his own training room in the converted garage at the rear of one of his shops.

To bring in some additional income, and to help to advertise the goods and services, he decides to run short training events for members of the public. Called Television and Video Explained, this is a half-day event run on Saturday mornings. It covers all the features of modern technology in the television and video field, including satellite systems. It has been designed to take away the mystery of all the jargon and to explain the costs.

Peter has a double-sided, A4 folded leaflet printed, advertising the events. These leaflets are available in all his shops. Registration is by filling in the form which is part of the leaflet, then handing this to any of the sales staff with the registration fee. Confirmation is by letter during the following week.

Peter runs his events on alternate Saturdays over a period of several months. They are very popular and the delegates find them informative and enjoyable. Peter also notices his shop sales increase as a result.

Several wrong turnings due to Charles's efforts

Charles, the building society manager, sends two of his counter staff, Geraldine and Victoria, to a one-day security workshop. This training event is designed to raise the counter staff's awareness of new trends in fraud and robbery.

The event is run by an external consultancy company. All booking arrangements are made over the phone and no written details are sent to the delegates. Charles has attended a previous event at the same venue, which is about 50 miles away. He has a good collection of OS maps and photocopies a map from these to provide a route for the two women. Photocopying the coloured maps results in a loss of most of the critical detail. Roads, rivers and railways all lose their identity. To add to the women's difficulties it's winter and they start their journey in the dark.

They arrive nearly an hour after the event starts, having made several wrong turnings. They have missed the introduction and coffee, and find it very hard to relax and take in what is being said.

On their return to the branch the women can only remember how difficult the journey was, and have learned very little about security measures.

DISCUSSION POINTS

1. Sometimes there can be several different training events at the same venue. Apart from providing decent sign-posting, what steps could you take to make sure the delegates start off in the right rooms?

2. You have organised a series of one-day events for people who want to learn about starting up small businesses at home. You have booked a venue for ten weeks in advance. For the first date you only have two bookings. The break-even point to make money is five delegates. What should you do?

3. Imagine you are a delegate at an event which involves a long car journey and overnight accommodation at the venue. List your top ten priorities to make your attendance enjoyable. Would these also help you with the objective of the event?

8
Running the Training Event

FINDING THE RIGHT TUTORS

A training event can be run by the person who designed the event, or by tutors who have had no involvement in the planning. Some typical situations are given below.

• There can be one tutor who introduces the event and takes all the sessions.

• There can be a leader who deals with the introduction and takes a selection of the sessions. A second tutor takes the remaining sessions.

• There can be a leader who is just there to make sure everything runs smoothly. Other tutors deal with most of the sessions, and guest speakers cover specialist subjects.

Improving the department with specialist help
A typical situation can be illustrated by using the Nesscliff Health Authority's team building event, which was introduced as an example in Chapter 3. The following people are involved in running the event.

Event leader
Simon Scarratt is a full-time training manager from the health authority's training department. He has a flair for making events run well, although he has no specialist technical or medical skills.

Tutor assisting event leader
Lynda Leyton is a full-time trainer from the training department. Simon is her manager. She has good presentation skills and is well liked by event delegates.

Guest speaker No 1
Jason Jones, speaking on problem solving, works in the health
authority's Quality and Change Management department. He has had
many years experience with total quality techniques, particularly in the
area of problem solving. He tends to be a little arrogant, and delegates
are never particularly relaxed when he's running a session, but there is
no suitable alternative with his particular skills.

Guest speaker No 2
Louise Raeburn, speaking on violent behaviour, lectures at the nearby
Baschurch University in the psychology department. She also runs a
consultancy offering assistance to companies dealing with the public.
Her specialist subject is human behaviour, and she offers practical advice
on how to deal with members of the public who are abusive or violent.

Matching the tutor to the session requirements
It makes an event more interesting if the tutors take turns to lead the
sessions. The various parts that make up the introduction session can
be divided between them as well. For example, Simon makes the
opening remarks then Lynda goes on to deal with the domestic issues.

Seeking the right tutors
Consider the following points when you are looking for the right
tutors.

1. Is he/she a qualified presenter or trainer?
2. Does he/she have specialist knowledge of the subject?
3. Can he/she be relied on to stick to allocated times?
4. Have there been good or bad reports from other events?
5. Does he/she have the confidence to face the delegates?
6. Do their specialist skills outweigh any shortcomings?

Confirming event details with tutors
If the tutors are in the same department as the event designer, then a
discussion about the training event will be sufficient to confirm all the
arrangements. For guest speakers and people brought in from other
departments, written confirmation is recommended. In either case the
following points need to be covered:

• date and venue
• directions to the venue
• location of the room

- time sessions are being run and when to arrive
- the objectives of the sessions
- what material will be available
- what material needs to be brought
- polite reminder to stick to time
- arrangements for payment of fees.

Many of these points can be covered by giving copies of the event paperwork to the tutor.

In our case study the event designer would write to both the guest speakers. A suitable letter for the second guest speaker is illustrated in Figure 28. It has been assumed that the event leader is also the event designer.

WORKING FROM THE SESSION INFORMATION

Let's see what the tutor can use to guide him or her through the event. The aim should be to work with the minimum amount of tutor information; the presentation will be better if the tutor works from his or her head, rather than from detailed notes.

Minimising the tutor material

The information given to the tutor will consist of:

- event objective
- event plan
- session sheets
- materials checklist
- delegate list
- material required for each session.

The last item will be everything that's recorded on the materials section of the session sheets. All of this will also be covered by the materials checklist. It will include everything from agendas for the delegates to OHP slides.

Running the event without a script

Using only the items listed above, the tutor can run the event session by session, keeping time with the details on the event plan. Look back at the picture of an event, illustrated in Figure 5, and you will see it's a simple, step-by-step approach. The key points are:

Simon Scarratt
Training Manager
Nesscliff Health Authority

Louise Raeburn
Dept of Psychology
Baschurch University   13.5.199X

Dear Louise

Team building event – Friday 24th March

Thank you for your offer of assistance at this training event. I can now confirm the final arrangements.

The event is to be held in the conference suite at the Nesscliff Resort Hotel. This is one mile north of the town on the A900, just before you get to the junction with the M96 motorway.

I have enclosed an agenda for the event, to let you see how your involvement fits into the overall plan.

Your first session starts at 2pm. I suggest you arrive just before we break for lunch at 1pm. I can then introduce you to the delegates and you can join us for lunch in the Jasmine Restaurant.

There are three sessions covering the general theme of abusive and violent behaviour. I have enclosed copies of the session sheets relating to each of these, which give details of times and the session objectives.

For the role-play session my assistant Lynda and I will take turns in playing the part of an abusive or violent customer. I enclose a list of the twelve situations we will be creating, which you may find helpful to have in advance.

There will be a video player with wide-screen TV, and an OHP available in the event room. As agreed will you please bring the video *Defending Yourself at Work* and your presentation slides.

As the success of this event will depend on completing a number of activities in one day I am reminding all tutors of the need to keep to the agenda times. Regarding the agreed fee of £200, please leave an invoice with Lynda at the end of the event.

I am looking forward to your involvement in our training event, and I am sure the delegates will find your contribution extremely helpful and informative.

Yours sincerely

Simon Scarratt

Fig. 28. Letter to a guest speaker.

1. Event plan is always visible to the tutor.
2. Timing of the event is kept on track by keeping an eye on the event plan.
3. Relevant session sheet is viewed to provide tutor with guidance to each session.
4. At end of session, session sheet is turned over to show next session sheet.

Using additional information

While the tutor is working through each session additional information will come from:

- his or her knowledge of the subject
- experience of previous events
- prompts from text on OHP slides and flip-charts
- summaries or script in workbooks.

Scripting the sessions

Sometimes the tutor will need a script to work from. A script can be required when:

- The tutors have no knowledge of the subject.
- The event is a trial or initial run.
- There are legal reasons such as health and safety.

Plenty of practice runs before the event will allow tutors to cover the script word for word, without having their heads down. Where scripts are being used the notes section of the session sheet should make reference to the script.

ENSURING MATERIALS ARE TO HAND

All the materials required for the event will be listed in the materials checklist. The tutor should always check the materials against the checklist in advance of the event. This is particularly important if someone else, for example the event designer, has packed the material and taken it to the venue.

Packing and unpacking the event material

If you are responsible for packing event material before the event, or unpacking it at the event:

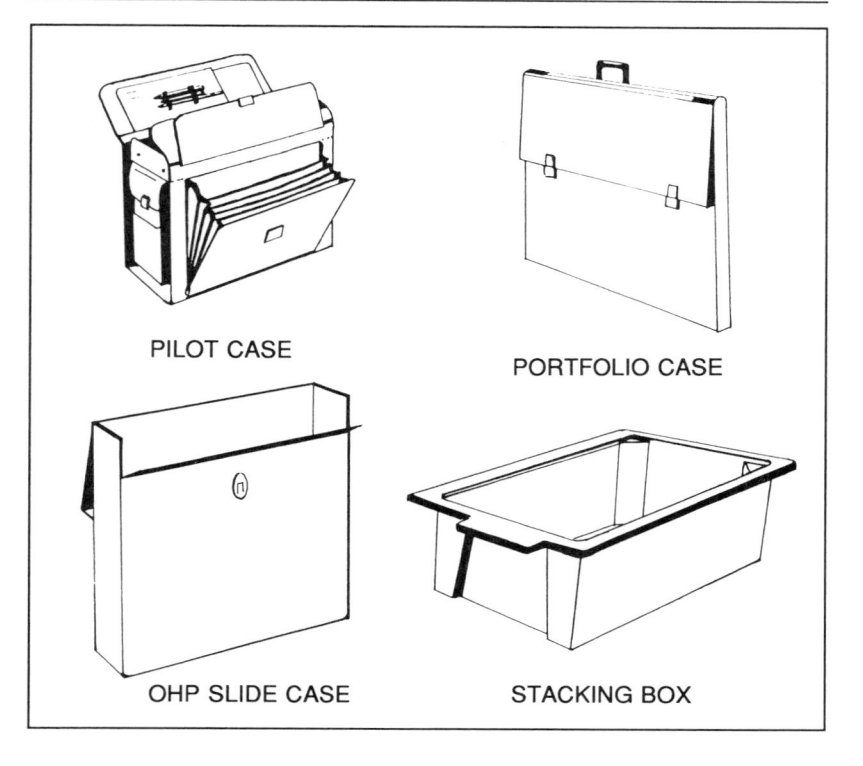

PILOT CASE

PORTFOLIO CASE

OHP SLIDE CASE

STACKING BOX

Fig. 29. Boxes and cases for event material.

- use suitable boxes or special carrying cases
- pack in good time for the event
- if possible recheck items just before leaving for the event
- test OHPs, video players, etc on arrival
- unpack at the venue, checking against the checklist
- lay out the material logically so it's to hand as the event progresses.

Some suitable boxes and cases to carry materials are illustrated in Figure 29.

Using the material
The details on the session sheets act as prompts for when material is to be used. This will be recorded in the materials and notes sections. Typically this will include:

– when the tutor needs to use OHP slides, for example during a presentation about the company balance sheets

– when a handout needs to be given to the delegates, for example giving out the agenda during an introduction session

– special set-ups, for example the smoke-filled room for delegates to try out breathing apparatus.

PRESENTING PROPERLY

The effectiveness of a training event is helped by good presentations by the tutors. Some people are natural presenters, but for most of us good presentation skills come with attention to key behaviours and a bit of practice.

Being a decent presenter
As a tutor at an event you should avoid habits that irritate the delegates. A distracted delegate will not learn effectively.

The top ten hints for effective presentation
1. Maintain eye contact with delegates.
2. Only attempt to make jokes if you're a natural comic.
3. Don't read from notes: prepare simple prompt lists.
4. Don't bore people with how good you are at your job.
5. Avoid annoying nervous habits, such as jingling the loose change in your pocket.
6. Support what you're saying with simple illustrations on a flip-chart or OHP.
7. Practise before the event and make sure length fits allocated slot.
8. Avoid using jargon.
9. Don't talk down to people.
10. Sound as though you believe in what you're saying.

Coping with nerves
Tutors do get nervous when they make a presentation or give a demonstration. This is only natural. It happens to the most experienced of presenters and even where the tutor knows all the delegates.

Recognising the value of nerves
– Everyone gets nervous; some are better than others at hiding it.
– Being anxious about an event will focus your mind on the important details and can have positive results.

Appearing relaxed
- Never have alcohol before giving a presentation.
- Talk in your normal voice: don't shout.
- Focus on someone at the back, a friend or another tutor.
- Make eye contact with the other delegates from time to time.
- Don't fiddle with things like your tie, or pens on the table.
- Suck a sweet before you start.
- Don't clench your fists or link your hands together.
- Sit down when using an OHP, and point out items on the slide with a pen – don't point at the screen.

Feel and look confident
- Dress smartly.
- Hair should be neat.
- Gentlemen: clean-shaven or tidy beard.
- Tie straight.
- Shoes clean.
- Ladies: don't overdo jewellery and make-up.
- If you need to wear glasses then wear them.
- Talk at your normal talking speed.
- Stand straight.
- Rest hand on flip-chart easel, lectern or back of chair.

Remembering what you want to say
- Use visual aids as prompts.
- Practise beforehand.
- Progress the subject logically.
- If you think you've forgotten something, leave it to the end; don't jump backwards and forwards through a subject.

DEALING WITH DIFFICULTIES

A well organised training event should run without any difficulties. However, unforeseen problems do sometimes occur. Let's look at what can be done to prevent them spoiling the event.

Arriving late

Delegates sometimes arrive late. It helps to have half or quarter of an hour when refreshments are available before the start time. Give out the telephone number of the venue so that delegates can let you know they're going to be late. If a delegate fails to arrive by the start time, you will have to decide when to start.

Start on time if:
- The general theme of the training is precision or efficiency, for example at a railway company training event.
- The event plan timing is known to have no slack in it.

Delay start by up to 15 minutes only if:
- The theme of the training is about caring for customers or staff.
- It's known that time can be made up during the event.

Running the event to the plan
If you find the event is running either in front or behind the times in the event plan, here's what you can do to bring it back on track.

Do
- Vary the lunch break accordingly.
- Introduce additional comfort breaks.
- Look ahead to other sessions which will be shorter or longer than time on plan.
- Help any delegate who's slowing things down.
- Remind guest speakers if they're over-running.
- Remain calm: the event timing is unlikely to be very far out by the time you get to the end.

Don't
- Allow questions from delegates to slow things down.
- Try to talk quicker or slower.
- Cut out refreshment breaks.
- Allow guest speakers to hog the show.
- Try to redesign the event half-way through.
- Panic.

Delivering delegates from difficulty
Here are typical situations where delegates can get into difficulty, and what a tutor can do to help.

Delegate	*Tutor*
Slower than the rest during practical sessions.	Sit with delegate and do some of the work yourself.
Can't lift heavy objects or cope physically during practical sessions.	Stand delegate to one side and ask them to watch the others. Ask delegate to take notes then

	give a short report back to everyone at the end of the session.
Taken ill.	Don't force him or her to stay. Contact family or manager and arrange for them to be taken home.
Finds out halfway through event that it's not what they wanted.	Ask them to continue to the end and to judge it against the eventual objective.

General rule for dealing with delegates in difficulties
Never push a delegates to one side, or criticise them in front of the others.

Putting down awkward delegates

Awkward delegates are easily dealt with if you have issued a set of ground rules at the start of an event, like those illustrated in Figure 9.

A delegate who tries to disrupt an event, by asking deliberately difficult questions or criticising the aims of the training, can be firmly but politely reminded of the ground rules.

All issues and disagreements can be dealt with between that delegate and the tutor during a break or over lunch. In practice, if challenged against the ground rules, the awkward delegate won't bother to discuss the matter further. His intention will have been to cause the tutors difficulties, rather than it being a genuine concern of his.

CHECKLIST FOR RUNNING TRAINING EVENTS

1. Find the right tutors
   (a) select suitable tutors
   (b) allocate to the sessions
   (c) written invitations to guest speakers.

2. Give tutors the session information
   (a) keep to a minimum
   (b) try to run without a script
   (c) tutor to use session materials as prompts
   (d) script only in special cases.

3. Make sure all materials are to hand
   (a) pack and unpack against materials checklist

(b) use suitable boxes and cases
(c) lay out material logically
(d) use material as per the details on session sheets.

4. Present each session properly
   (a) avoid irritating habits which upset the delegates
   (b) take steps to cope with nerves.

5. Deal with difficulties
   (a) decide what to do if delegates are late
   (b) keep event running to overall plan times
   (c) help delegates in difficulties
   (d) deal effectively with awkward delegates.

CASE STUDIES

Joyce's confidence is dented

Michael sends Joyce, a team manager in the accounts department to a one-day event called Assertiveness for Female Managers.

One of the sessions, confidence building, is led by a male guest speaker. He talks for an hour, walking up and down at the front of the room, reading from notes without looking up. His movements are so predictable that Joyce finds herself counting the number of paces he takes each time he crosses the room. The delegates are all female, but the speaker's tone is one of male superiority.

There is no practical follow-up session, and Joyce comes away remembering only the number of paces the guest speak took to cross the room.

Michael agrees to help. He asks his own training manager, Jackie, to design and run a half-day confidence building event. It is designed around a commercial video which comes with workbooks and notes. This time there are no problems and the event objective is successfully met.

Jenny steps into Peter's shoes

Peter has run several Saturday morning open day training events in the training room. He is going on two weeks holiday, so he passes the responsibility of tutor over to Jenny, one of his sales assistants.

Jenny sits in on the last event run by Peter before he goes away. She takes notes of the key points in each session. Using these notes, and the event plan and session sheets, Jenny is able to run the next event. She's nervous, but takes steps to keep this under control. It helps that Peter has told her he still gets nervous himself, even though he's run the event a dozen times.

Jenny runs two events in Peter's absence and they are just as effective as when he runs them.

No fumbling after Geraldine checks in

Each year a building society branch is picked to run a one-day training event for the other branches, at a hotel near the area office. That office chooses the event objective, designs the event and supplies all the event material. The purpose is to give a branch manager and team the experience of running a training event.

It's the turn of Charles's branch, and a few days ahead of the event he goes to the area office to pick up the event material. A material checklist is provided, so he's able to make sure everything is included.

At the venue Geraldine unpacks the material. She uses the materials checklist again, just to make sure everything is included. She lays the material out along a table behind the tutors' table, in an order which matches that of the sessions.

When the event is run there's no fumbling for handouts or OHP slides. Everything is very easy to find. At the end of the event all the delegates agree it was well organised and ran very smoothly.

DISCUSSION POINTS

1. You're in charge of a five-day training event in a hotel with overnight accommodation. All the delegates have been sent by their companies at a cost of over £1,000 each. At the end of day two one of the delegates tells you he's finding the event too difficult and he thinks he'll pack his bags and leave in the morning. Would you let him leave, or try to persuade him to stay till the end?

2. You're running a one-day event for a large group of people, and the guest speaker has telephoned you two days before the event to say he's ill and can't attend. The session being taken by the guest speaker included a video, and it was to have made an important contribution to the event. What could you do to ensure the event went ahead and the event objective was still achieved?

3. Tutors are recommended to sit down while using an OHP and to point to the items on the slide with a pen. Alternatively, the tutor could move over to the screen to point to the projected image. To change to the next slide the tutor will then have to go back to the projector, meaning they move about a lot more. What problems will this cause for the delegates and for the tutor?

9
Building on Success

MEASURING THE RESULTS

The success of a training event is measured by comparing the end result with what the event set out to achieve. This measurement is done during the closing session of the event. Look back at the diagram illustrated in Figure 2 to see how this fits into the event flowchart.

Closing the event
In the event plan illustrated in Figure 11 thirty minutes has been allocated to the **closing session**. There will be a session sheet for this, covering the following items:

1. Summing up by tutor
   (a) thank delegates for attending
   (b) thank delegates for working so hard
   (c) go through any outstanding issues recorded during the event
   (d) say what will happen with any issues that have not been resolved during the event.

2. Restating the event objective
   (a) display the event objective
   (b) read through it to remind delegates why they have been to the event.

3. Review of event. Use a review sheet to measure success.

4. Closing remarks
   (a) issue certificates of attendance
   (b) delegates reminded to pick up all their papers and personal items
   (c) say goodbye and wish delegates a safe journey.

EVENT REVIEW

1. **Event objective**. Do you agree that the overall
    objective has been met by this training event?   Yes/No
    If no please say why:

2. **Venue**. Was the venue a suitable place for the
    event?   Yes/No
    If no please say why:

3. **Accommodation**. Did the accommodation meet
    your requirements?   Yes/No
    If no please say why:

4. **Overall score**.

    Please give a mark out of 10 for how effective you feel the training has
    been.

                                                            _____

5. **Likes and dislikes**. Please give one thing that you liked and one
    thing that you disliked about the event:

Name ....   **Phone No**. ....

You may leave off your name, but it will help if we are able to contact
you to discuss any important points you have made. If you have any
other points you wish to make please write these on the back of this
form. Thank you for your cooperation.

Fig. 30. An event review sheet.

Reviewing the event

For item 3 of the closing session an **event review** sheet is used, as
illustrated in Figure 30. This can be used either by:

- asking each delegate to fill one in during the closing session
- having questions displayed on a flip-chart, then going round the
  room for individual answers.

Taking action on results
If there are any serious concerns about any part of the event, the delegates will raise these during the review. Changes that may need to be made for future events can be identified as follows.

Meeting the objective: question 1
The target should be at least 80 per cent. This means if there were ten delegates you can only have two recording a no. If more than two say the objective wasn't met the designer will need to make changes to the event before it's run again. The delegate's comments will help pinpoint where the problem is.

Venue and accommodation: questions 2 and 3
A number of negative comments about a hotel, for example, will need to be taken up with the hotel manager before it's used again. Or another hotel chosen.

Overall score: question 4
1. Add up all the scores
2. Divide total by No of delegates
3. Multiply answer by 10

This gives an average score for effectiveness. You should get a score of at least 85 per cent.

Likes and dislikes: question 5
This will highlight any organisational good or bad points. Delegates will tend to praise or complain about the venue or accommodation rather than the content of the training event. And these are important, because they can help or hinder meeting the training event objective.

Assessing the effectiveness at the workplace
For internally organised training events it's possible to find out how effective the training has been back at the workplace. One method of doing this is to write to the delegates two months after they have completed their training. A typical internal memo is illustrated in Figure 31.

Filing the results
The results of success measurement, at the end of the event and back at the workplace, should be held in section 9 of the designer's file (see Figure 22).

INTERNAL MEMO

To: Joe Sparks   From: Jeff James
Service Dept   Training Mgr

Dear Joe

You recently attended a one-day course: Handling Customer
Complaints. The objective of this course was to familiarise you and
other members of the team with the new complaint handling
procedures, so that you would be able to log complaints on the
database, and deal with customers on all aspects of the company's
products and services, including writing replies.

I would be very interested to have your views as to how effective you
feel the training was.

Comments

Signed   date

Please return this memo with your comments to the training
department.

Yours sincerely

Jeff James

Fig. 31. A method of assessing training effectiveness.

ISSUING A CERTIFICATE

Delegates should each be given a training certificate at the end of the
event. An example is illustrated in Figure 32. This is to take back to
their workplace as proof of attendance. Certificates should be kept with
other personal records.

Training certificates can easily be drawn up on a personal computer.
Use an A4 size; frames are available if the delegate wants to put the
certificate on the office wall. Photocopy on coloured paper, which
looks more professional. The tutor should sign each copy individually.

Certificate of Attendance

This is to certify that

...*Joyce Defries*.....

has attended the training event

Confidence Building

at the Borough Council Training School

on...*25 March 9X*...

Signed.*Jackie James*. Tutor   Date.*25/4/9X*.

Fig. 32. An example of a training certificate.

CLIFTON COUNTY CONSTABULARY
Nuisance Call Handling

Training Test Paper   **1 HOUR**

Candidate's name.......................... Station/dept ....

Part 1. Multiple choice   10 minutes

(Use the ten-question/three-choice layout as illustrated in Figure 13, but make all answer choices serious).
Total marks 20

Part 2. Short answers   20 minutes

Give the correct response to the following enquiries by members of the public. Use no more than twenty words to describe the action you would take. Write in space provided.

1. Case no. 1. Mr Jones calls in to the local station to report vandalism to his car which occurred outside his house. He also says his wife has received several recent phone calls from a stranger accusing him (Mr Jones) of having an affair with one of the young girls at the bank where he works.

    ....

    ....

2. Case no. 2. Same layout as no. 1 and so until case no. 5.

Total marks 50

Part 3. Written exercise   30 minutes

You have brought in Mr Raymond Jacks for questioning in relation to alleged nuisance telephone calls to a Ms Patricia Bullimore. You have a list of calls supplied by BT and a statement from Ms Bullimore. Copies of these documents are appended to this paper.

Mr Jacks has responded to your questions and has admitted to making the calls to Ms Bullimore.

Write out what you could consider an appropriate statement from Mr Jacks, so that you could ensure a successful prosecution in court.

Record your answer on the paper provided. You may start by making rough notes, then delete these with a diagonal line.

Total marks 30

Fig. 33. An exam paper layout.

SETTING AN EXAM

Some training events will need to include an exam. Delegates who pass the exam will be given a certificate which is proof of competence in the subject rather than just attendance of the event. An exam will typically be used at events involving:

- legal matters such as health and safety
- accreditation to do specialist work such as an official company trainer.

Including an exam

An exam would be the last working session in the event plan, coming just before the closing session. An example of a suitable exam paper layout is illustrated in Figure 33.

- Designer should seek advice from an expert in the subject to help with setting the questions.

- Marking of the papers should be after the event, with the results sent on to the delegates.

- Use the classroom layout for the exam room.

- Set an attainable but high pass mark, typically 85 per cent.

CHECKLIST FOR MEASURING SUCCESS

The following points should be considered when measuring the success of training.

1. Include an event review in the closing session.

2. Use a review sheet to assess:
    (a) meeting the objective
    (b) venue
    (c) accommodation
    (d) overall score
    (e) likes and dislikes.

3. Take appropriate action on results.

4. If possible assess effectiveness at workplace.

5. File results in designer's file.

6. Issue delegates with a certificate.

7. Include an exam if appropriate.

CASE STUDIES

High scores despite no good beer

From the review of the local authority two-day team building event at Overton Hall, the following results were recorded.

1. Event Objective
The four delegates, including Michael the department head, all said the objective had been met.

2. Venue
Everyone liked Overton Hall and said it was a good choice for the venue.

3. Accommodation
Michael and two of the other delegates said that the accommodation met their requirements. Sandra Scott answered no to this question because she had a number of problems with her room.

4. Overall score
Scores were as follows:

Michael Brown	9
Joyce Defries	9
Sandra Scott	8
David McBride	10
Total	36 ÷ 4 x 10% = 90 per cent

5. Likes and dislikes

	Liked	**Disliked**
Michael Brown	organisation	travelling between venue and accommodation
Joyce Defries	lunches	event room too warm
Sandra Scott	team spirit	shower didn't work in her room at hotel
David McBride	atmosphere of Overton Hall	poor range of beers in hotel bar

Jackie, who organised the training part of the event, was pleased with the results and judged the event to have been successful and effective.

Joyce, who organised the venue and accommodation, said she would try to have the venue and accommodation at the same site for the next event. A hotel with conference facilities and appropriate old world charm would be suitable.

Peter's packs raise sales

In the closing session of his Saturday morning training event, Television and Video Explained, Peter hands out a pack of information to the delegates. It contains:

- a business card giving the addresses and phone numbers of his shops

- a summary of key points covered at the event

- a current price list of the equipment and accessories available in his shops, with details of credit schemes

- a training certificate with the delegate's name and signed by Peter, or Jenny his substitute.

The delegates are pleased to receive this pack and show it to their friends. This leads to more people attending the event and to higher sales in Peter's shops.

Work wins the war

The building society area manager sends Charles on a three-day residential course, Winning the War at Work, run by an external consultancy. This is the final attempt to get Charles more involved in the running of his building society branch.

The area manager has been on this event herself and knows it's all about managers getting fully involved with running a team. The course is very intense, with evening sessions and difficult role-play situations. During the afternoon of the final day there is a two-hour exam.

A week after Charles returns from the event he learns he has passed the exam. The area manager now knows that Charles is fully aware of what's expected of him at the branch.

The situation at the branch changes dramatically. Charles comes out of his office and spends most of his time with the counter staff and gets fully involved with the customers.

DISCUSSION POINTS

1. You are recommended to review the success of an event during the closing session. Do you think giving the delegates a questionnaire to take away and send in later would work as well?

2. If an event takes longer than planned, do you think a review during the closing session will have as much value as a review from one that finished on time?

3. Imagine you have designed a fairly long training event, with at least ten sessions. As a result of an assessment at the workplace, two months later, it's found that the delegates are having difficulty with just one area of the work. What action would you take?

4. What other activities in a training event could be marked and used instead of, or added to, the marks from an exam?

Glossary

Brainstorming. A method of generating ideas which can be worked on by the delegates during subsequent sessions. Useful for identifying problems that are preventing staff doing their work properly.

Client. The person who identifies the training need and then defines what the training should achieve.

Delegate. A person who attends the training event and receives the training.

Designer. The person who plans the training event on behalf of the client.

Designer's file. A file containing information about the planning of the training, from the client requirements through to the measurement of success.

Domestics. Part of the introductory session, when the delegates are informed about fire alarms, location of toilets, etc.

Event. Training event is the term used to describe all types of training courses and seminars.

Event plan. A list of all working and non-working sessions, with their duration, start and finish times. The tutor uses the plan as a timetable to keep the training event running to time.

Ground rules. A set of rules introduced at the start of the event which helps with timekeeping and allows the tutors to deal with difficult delegates.

Handouts. Papers, workbooks, or other material, given to the delegates during the event, either to work with during a session or for reference purposes.

Material. Items a tutor needs to use during the event. This can include videos, scripts, tools, machinery, handouts, overhead projectors, etc.

Objectives. The event objective is a written statement saying what the training is to achieve. Each session of the event also has an individual objective.

Reviews. At various stages of the design of a training event the designer will have discussions with the client to ensure the event will meet the client requirements. There is also a review during the last session with the delegates, to measure the success of the training.

Role-play. The delegates are given parts to play in imaginary situations, simulating real situations they will experience back at their workplace.

Seminar. A training event with a high level of delegate participation, such as discussions and problem solving. Less formal than a training course.

Session. A training event is made up of a series of sessions. Some will be working sessions, which each have their own objective, for example learning to use a computer. There will also be non-working sessions like refreshment breaks.

Syndicate exercise. The delegates divide into smaller groups, often in rooms separate from the main training room. They then work on exercises given to them by the tutor.

Team building. Training to improve the effectiveness of a group of people who work together.

Tutor. The person who presents the training event. There may be more than one tutor, and often guest speakers are used to run some of the sessions.

Workbook. A document handed out to the delegates, which contains information and written exercises.

Further Reading

The following books give further guidance to tutors on the presentation aspect of training events.

Successful Presentation (In a Week), Malcolm Peel (Institute of Management, Hodder and Stoughton, 1992). Book plus audio cassette.

Effective Presentation, Anthony Jay (Institute of Management, Pitman Publishing, 1993).

Effective Presentation Skills, Steve Mandel (Kogan Page, 1987).

How to Give an Effective Seminar, Watson, Pardso and Tomovic (Kogan Page, 1994). (Brit. edition). Information about seminar-style events.

How to Master Public Speaking, Ann Nicholls (How To Books, 3rd edition 1995).

Winning Presentations: How to Sell Your Ideas and Yourself, Ghassan Hasbani (How To Books, 1996). A step-by-step guide to presentation skills and techniques.

Useful Addresses

VISUAL AIDS AND OTHER MATERIAL

Catalogues of training material, from flip-chart easels to files for delegates, are available from the following suppliers.

Niceday Ltd, Niceday House, Greenwich Way, Andover, Hampshire SP10 4JZ. Tel: (01264) 333399. Fax: (01264) 344000. Suppliers of the Niceday range of materials. Formerly W H Smith Business Supplies.

Nobo Visual Aids, Alder Close, Eastbourne, Sussex, BN23 6QB. Tel: (01323) 641521. Fax: (01323) 410328. Nobo organise presentation skills training events as part of the promotion of the their products.

Office World Superstores. Freephone: (0900) 5000 24. Freefax: (0800) 24 5000. Supermarket-style warehouses with over forty stores in the UK.

TRAINING VIDEOS AND ASSOCIATED MATERIAL

Video Arts Ltd, Dumbarton House, 68 Oxford Street, London W1N 0LH. Tel: (0171) 637 7288. Fax: (0171) 580 8103. Video Arts specialises in the use of humour to emphasise key points. Foreign language variations also available.

BBC for Business, Woodlands, 80 Wood Lane, London W12 0TT. Tel: (0181) 576 2361. Fax: (0181) 576 2867. There are thirty-eight preview centres in the UK where their products can be viewed free of charge, and product distributors in twenty other countries.

Gower Publishing Limited, Customer Service, Gower House, Croft Road, Aldershot, Hampshire GU11 3HR. Tel: (01252) 317700. Fax:

(01252) 343151. Their training resources catalogue includes videos and other material such as team games and role-play kits.

GUIDANCE ON THE USE OF COMPUTERS

Display Screen Equipment work – Guidance on Regulations, Health and Safety Executive (HMSO, 1992). The correct use of display screen equipment.

Data Protection Registrar, Springfield House, Water Lane, Wilmslow, Cheshire SK9 5AX. Tel: (01625) 535777. You need to register for the storage of personal details of delegates, such as names and addresses.

Index